BROTHERS

ALSO BY VERNA J. DOZIER

The Dream of God

She Has Done a Beautiful Thing:
Women in the New Testament (Audio)

Discovering the Whole Story:
Biblical Narrative through the Church Year (Audio)

ALSO BY JAMES R. ADAMS

So You Think You're Not Religious?:
A Thinking Person's Guide to the Church

Verna J. Dozier   James R. Adams

SISTERS AND BROTHERS

Reclaiming a Biblical Idea of Community

COWLEY PUBLICATIONS

Cambridge ◆ *Boston*
Massachusetts

Published in the United States of America by Cowley Publications, a division of the Society of St. John the Evangelist. No portion of this book may be reproduced, stored in or introduced into a retrieval system, or transmitted, in any form or by any means— including photocopying— without the prior written permission from the publishers, except in the case of brief quotations embodied in critical articles and reviews.

International Standard Book Number: 1-56101-076-6
Library of Congress Number: 93-2755

Library of Congress Cataloging-in-Publication Data

Dozier, Verna J.
    Sisters and brothers : reclaiming a biblical idea of community / Verna J. Dozier, James R. Adams.
        p. cm.
    Includes bibliographical references.
    ISBN 1-56101-076-6 (alk. paper)
    1. Women in the Bible. 2. Sex role—Biblical teaching. 3. Sex role—Religious aspects—Christianity. 4. Men (Christian theology)—Biblical teaching. 5. Women (Christian theology)—Biblical teaching. I. Adams, James R., 1934- . II. Title.
BS680.W7D695 1993
261.8'343—dc20   93-2755

Unless otherwise noted, all scriptural quotations are taken from the New Revised Standard Version of the Bible.

Grateful acknowledgment is made to Dory Previn and Pawprint Music for permission to include the lyric "did jesus have a baby sister?"

Cowley Publications
28 Temple Place
Boston, MA 02111

For the people of St. Mark's

Acknowledgments

This little book began as a summer study course that we called "The Lost Sister," in which we wanted to explore the sister-brother stories in the Bible as a possible metaphor and guide for relationships between women and men. In our opinion, this task has become difficult because over the centuries the church has frequently lost track of the sisters.

In the course Verna retold the stories of women in the Hebrew Scriptures whose lives were overshadowed by their more famous brothers—Miriam, the sister of Moses, and Tamar, the sister of Absalom—and of the New Testament women who had acted as sisters to Jesus and to St. Paul. Jim filled in the background for the stories and provided information about the origins of some of the more puzzling words. More than half of the time in each session, however, was spent in discussion, partly in small groups and partly with the two of us present.

As we have developed the ideas that emerged from this course, we have discovered that the two of us have very different ways of perceiving, thinking, and writing. We have tried to harmonize our contrasting styles in order to avoid jarring transitions between our individual contributions. We may not have been totally successful in meeting this challenge, but we have both enjoyed the excuse for spending time together. We have collaborated on many projects in the past and have always found our joint ventures to be mutually rewarding.

We want to thank the people of St. Mark's Church, Capitol Hill in Washington, DC, for making the project possible. The wardens and vestry agreed for Jim to take several mornings a week to write, and they provided the computer support that was necessary. We particularly want to thank Steve Beste for coming to the rescue when Jim's computer broke down at a critical stage in revising the work. Finally, we offer our appreciation to those people who joined us in the initial discussions of the sister-brother imagery. They not only stimulated our thinking but also gave us the benefit of their insights.

Betty Smith and Mildred Wheat, the St. Mark's secretaries, also deserve our thanks for finding time in their busy schedules to print and copy the numerous drafts and revisions.

Cynthia Shattuck, our editor at Cowley Publications, once again proved herself to be a demanding taskmaster; the final product would have been quite different without her suggestions and critique. We are both pleased to have had the opportunity of working with her for a second time.

Jim Adams
Verna Dozier
Washington, DC

TABLE OF CONTENTS

Priscilla
The Sisters Disappear

The Trouble with Families
Equality, Justice, Intimacy
Women and Men in Partnership
Organizing as Sisters and Brothers
"The Least of These My Sisters and
    Brothers"
Joining the New Family

Introduction

Jesus replied, "Who is my mother, and who are my brothers?" And pointing to his disciples, he said, "Here are my mother and my brothers! For whoever does the will of my Father in heaven is my brother and sister and mother."
(Matthew 12:48-50)

All over the world people are breaking out of the conventional roles assigned to men and women. Women and men have been thrown together in offices and church organizations at a time when they have witnessed the de facto repeal of many ancient rules governing the interaction of the sexes. How are women and men to treat each other? What is the appropriate attitude to be held by one half of humanity toward the other half when they are not linked by bonds of blood or marriage?

Because of the uncertainty created by this social upheaval, women and men in the church are being forced to reexamine their ways of thinking about each other as well as to readjust their ways of treating each other. As roles assigned to women and men shift in confusing ways, many Christians are becoming ever more rigid in their defense of the same conventional social arrangements that Jesus challenged. They uphold the ideal of the "Christian family" in which men dominate women without seeming to notice that Jesus had nothing positive to say about such a system. In fact, what little Jesus had to say about natural families was quite negative. For example: "I have come to set a man against his father, and a daughter against her mother, and a daughter-in-law against her mother-in-law."[1] Other church people, in attempting to respond faithfully to new conditions, may not be content to fall back on familiar patterns of behavior: mother-son, father-daughter, suitor-sweetheart, or seducer-victim. They may also be unwilling to deny any differences between women and men and to pretend that we are all "just the guys." They may actually be ready for a biblical metaphor that will help redefine appropriate relationships between men and women in a Christian community, a redefinition they can take with them into their homes and offices.

Jesus of Nazareth offered a radical metaphor by which women and men might find a way of relating to one another. He told his followers that they were all his sisters and brothers and that, therefore, they were brothers and sisters to each other. Matthew's gospel has Jesus make this response during a teaching ministry that has attracted such large crowds that his family cannot get near him, and they send word to him that they are there. Someone delivers the message that his mother and his brothers are standing outside, wanting to speak to him. He sends back this astonishing answer, an answer recorded by three of the gospels in much the same way and in much the same words:

> "Who is my mother, and who are my brothers?" And pointing to his disciples, he said, "Here are my mother and my brothers! For whoever does the will of my Father in heaven is my brother and sister and mother."[2]

When all three gospels agree on a response of Jesus, we have an indication that we are dealing with an authentic fragment from the memory of the earliest Christian community.

In some churches today people call each other brother or sister, but more often than not they ignore the radical implications of what Jesus proposed. In fact, the way the terms are employed implies rank instead of equality. The brothers are in charge, and the sisters must accept their lower status. Instead of challenging the norms of society, even churches that use the family language are simply reflecting what, until recently, have been acceptable social arrangements.

An anthropologist once noted that successful men today have much in common with dominant male baboons. Both demonstrate their status by surrounding themselves with compliant females. The senator has his bevy of attractive young aides, the scientist his research assistants, the basketball star his fans, the doctor his nurses and technicians. In other cultures, powerful men have acquired wives and concubines. The failure of the proposal Jesus made for an alternative to the usual system is perhaps understandable, for he was protesting customs that were certainly ancient, nearly universal, and arguably "natural." The idea that men and women should treat each other as sisters and brothers runs counter to deeply ingrained attitudes.

The best way to change attitudes, however, is to change our use of metaphors. "Change a metaphor, change the world," said a poet and teacher and friend of James Autry, president of the magazine group of the Meredith Corporation. In *Love and Profit*, his delightful book about "the art of caring leadership," Autry has pointed out the trouble American businessmen have created for themselves by their use of sports metaphors. Not only have they made women feel excluded from the "team," they have also created an approach to business "in which there must be winners and losers, in which there are stars who play and benchwarmers who watch."[3] By changing the metaphor from sports to community or fellowship, a manager can open up new ways of thinking for the organization.

People who take seriously the sister-brother metaphor will begin to see each other differently. Men and women will develop another way of meeting each other and being with each other. They may at first find it difficult to think about each other as sisters and brothers, but the church offers people a place to explore the metaphor before they face the challenges of work and social organizations.

In looking to the metaphor that Jesus introduced, people will find themselves exploring new territory, since "the sister" has retreated into the background.[4] In searching for her, it helps to know something about the Greek language used by the Christian communities that produced the writings we call the New Testament. In Greek the word for sister was *adelphe* (pronounced ahd-el-fáy) and for brother, *adelphos*. Both words mean literally "from the womb" and originally meant from the same womb. When the first Christian writers referred to the followers of Jesus collectively they used *adelphoi*. *Adelphoi* is the plural of the masculine form, but it generally includes the feminine as well. In much the same fashion, when *adelphos* stands alone and the context of the sentence does not make clear the sex of the person, it can mean "brother or sister." In modern English, as in the Greek of the New Testament, the masculine often includes both men and women, but a feminine form is available for referring to women in particular. For example, all the members of a performing company are called "actors" but a person referring to a woman on the stage could appropriately identify her as an "actress." The practice of using the masculine form of a word to include the feminine, however, creates a problem: it is easy to lose sight of the feminine.

John's gospel uses the womb imagery used by Jesus in a way that does not risk being taken as exclusively masculine. This gospel, the only one that does not record the radical redefinition of family remembered by the other three, includes a story that sheds light on the way the early Christians understood the sister-brother metaphor: the story of Nicodemus.[5]

Nicodemus, a Pharisee and a leader of the Jews, has come to Jesus by night, obviously intrigued by this audacious young rabbi but not yet willing to risk his reputation by openly associating with him. They hold a conversation that was confusing to Nicodemus and to the community gathered in Jesus's name almost two thousand years later. Jesus tells him that no one can see the kingdom of God without being "born again," as the King James Version has it, or being "born from above" as the newer versions translate the expression. All versions record the complete bafflement of Nicodemus at the idea of another birth. "How can anyone be born after having grown old?" Nicodemus logically asks. "Can one enter a second time into the mother's womb and be born?" No, but Jesus knew about another parent, the Creator of us all. Jesus called the Creator "Father," but the literalizing of that poetic image has encouraged theologies destructive to half of the children born from the same spiritual womb, the female half.

To recover the full power of the sister-brother imagery in the Bible, we must pay particular attention to the feminine side of the equation, which tradition has often ignored or repressed. We begin with an attempt to discover the attitude Jesus held toward the women he called his sisters and then turn to the sister and brother stories of the Hebrew Scriptures that may have informed the early Christian understanding of the metaphor. After a look at how women and men lived and worked together in the churches guided by St. Paul, we will see how the brother-sister metaphor can make a difference in our churches and in the world.

Bible Study

We have offered in this book what we learned from our experience of looking again to see what the ancient records might offer us. We hope this book will encourage you to begin, or to continue, your exploration of the Scriptures. Since we hope that you will study the Bible and not this book, we have provided an extended Bible study that focuses on the theme of each chapter; it is found at the end of the book. As you approach your study of the Bible, we suggest you consider the process we have found helpful in this kind of endeavor.

A familiar prayer says that God caused "all Holy Scriptures to be written for our learning." Learning from Scripture, however, takes disciplined work.

The ancient Hebrews believed that God was present and active in every event of their lives—"In him we live and move and have our being." Understanding the ways of God was not automatic. The events of history gave a clue, but those events had to be interpreted, and interpretations varied. As the prophet Isaiah said: "For my thoughts are not your thoughts, nor are your ways my ways, says the Lord. For as the heavens are higher than the earth, so are my ways higher than your ways and my thoughts than your thoughts."[6] You had to walk humbly on the holy ground. The earliest writings included in the Hebrew Scriptures have one view of history; a chronicler writing at a later age saw things differently. In the gospels, Matthew saw it one way; Luke saw it another. The actions of God in history go on, and the interpretations go on. The Bible is written for our learning. Learning is a continuous process.

In learning from the ancient writings, it is important to distinguish Bible study from Bible reading. Bible study and Bible reading are both good, but they each have different processes and different purposes. Confusing them does each an injustice because the peculiar values of each can be lost.

Bible reading is a liturgical act. It occurs when the community gathers for worship. It reminds us of our common heritage and that we are members one of another. It assures us we are in a familiar place and a safe place; we know what is going to happen. Bible reading is a devotional act. We do it alone, although we often do it in the same place and at the same time that other people are engaged in the same devotional act. Often the passages chosen are familiar ones. We are reassured, eased, delighted. The experience of Bible reading can take place in a group where the people are all of one mind, a company of sojourners on the same journey.

Bible study, on the other hand, is potentially a disturbing activity. It is a wrestling with the text. It is a dangerous activity. New ground can open up before you. The foundations can be shaken. Before undertaking such an upsetting commitment, members of a Bible study group should ground themselves with an overview of the entire story, from Genesis to Revelation. They could prepare for the study of particular passages by reading together a liturgical setting of the drama of redemption, such as Eucharistic Prayer C in the Book of Common Prayer, or they could read the introductory chapter to a Bible study guide, such as "The Story of the Bible" in *The Bible for Today's Church* by Robert Bennett and O. C. Edwards.

Bible study can be done alone, but it presupposes a community of people with the same commitment to study, a group willing to test the results of their work with each other. The group can be as small as three and should be no larger than twelve. Large classes can be subdivided for certain portions of each session.

Having several different translations of the Scriptures available can help a group appreciate some of the nuances of the original Greek or Hebrew text. For example, the New Revised Standard Version of the Bible uses a great variety of expressions for *adelphos* and *adelphoi*, "from the same womb," when the words are used as a metaphor and are not to be taken literally. It is helpful to compare the King James Version's use of "brother" and "brethren" with the gender neutral word or phrase that appears at the same point in the NRSV. Both versions studied side by side will help provide a clearer picture of life in the early church than either translation could when used by itself.

The Bible study will be most valuable to the participants if they will do some work at home between sessions. To guide people in their initial study, we have provided some questions that we hope will free them from previous assumptions about the Bible and encourage them to examine carefully what the texts actually say. The group discussion questions for each chapter have no right or wrong answers. They are designed to elicit thoughtful reflection, encouraging people to identify what disturbed them or pleased them about what they have found in a passage of Scripture.

Whether people do their initial study of a passage at home or after gathering, each person would do well to write down not only the answers to the preparation questions, but also any additional questions that passage raises for them. These additional questions can be categorized in three ways.

Type 1 questions ask about the dictionary meaning of the words. These questions can be triggered by the translators' choice of words. For example, in Romans 16:1, why does the KJV call Phoebe a "servant" while the NRSV gives her the title "deacon" with the alternative "minister"? Type 2 questions ask what was going on in the life of the community when the events of the passage first took place and what was going on in the life of the community at the time the passage was preserved. Type 3 questions ask what the passage says to the church, the people of God, today. What does it say to me as a member of the church?

We think that the Bible study should take no more than two hours. When the group gets together, allow the first fifteen minutes for people to talk about what they discovered in looking for answers to the preparation questions and about how the passage struck them. This is not a time for people to challenge one another, but a time for each one to be heard. Then move on to a careful consideration of the text using some or all of the group discussion suggestions we have provided. Be aware of the Type 1 and Type 2 questions that may have occurred to the participants, always being ready to ask: "What did you learn?" and "What do you still want to know?" Then move on to the Type 3 questions. Type 3 questions are different from the other two types. Only the individual student can answer these questions because the answers are personal. The last part of the period is for letting each person describe what they have gained as a result of their study and conversation. Any comment from another member of the group—except for clarification of a position or appreciation for a new idea—is usually inappropriate.

The suggestions for discussion that we have posed for the first three chapters concentrate on the biblical texts, while the questions for Chapter 4 shift the emphasis to the lives of the participants. They will be examining not only their individual behavior, but the corporate behavior of the institutions in which they live and work, including the church. The best test of the Bible study's value will be found in the degree to which people have a positive effect on the world around them.

We trust that by exploring the sister-brother imagery found in the Bible you will come to a fuller understanding of what Jesus had in mind for his followers, and we hope that understanding will enrich your life.

Endnotes

1. Matt. 10:35
2. Matt. 12:46-50; Mark 3:31-35; Luke 8:19-21.
3. James A. Autry, *Love and Profit: The Art of Caring Leadership* (New York: William Morrow, 1991), p. 71.
4. Edith Deed's 1955 study, *All the Women of the Bible*, is a comprehensive though traditional listing of all the stories about the women in the Bible. The author divides her book into two parts, "Searching Studies of Women in the Foreground" and "Chronological Listings of Nameless Women in the Background." Under the latter category she lists daughters, wives, mothers, widows, and other unnamed women. Sisters is not even a category. Under the heading "Other Unnamed Women" she lists Nereus's sister included in Paul's salutation to many in the church at Rome, but she omits entirely Paul's sister mentioned in Acts 23:16 and Jesus's sisters mentioned in the gospels.
5. John 3:1-10
6. Is. 55:8-9

Chapter 1

A New Family

M en and women have as much difficulty relating to one another now, at the close of the twentieth century, as they did at the beginning of the first century when Jesus of Nazareth offered a radical redefinition of the family: "Whoever does the will of my Father in heaven is my brother and sister." Here was a new possibility for freeing women and men from the oppressive weight of tradition that assigned them dominating or demeaning roles in society. Now they could enjoy the same kind of rough equality that exists between sisters and brothers in a young family.

Jesus had a vision of a partnership between men and women in a community that was caring, supportive, and challenging. It was not to be a relationship of lovers, spouses, or mentors, for these are not relationships between equals or friends. Jesus revealed within the community of those who followed him a new possibility for human life through the brother-sister relationship, which was not a threat to nor in competition with any other relationship, but a new possibility for men and women discovered in community and lived out in all the world—the workplace, the political arena, all the sectors where men and women interact.

By the time the community established by Jesus had become an institution, however, the desire for order and respectability had all but eliminated the new possibility for human interaction. When the Christian church chose to worship Jesus instead of following him, it tamed much of what was threateningly radical in this disturbing person. Christians were no longer willing to offend their neighbors by encouraging independence in women and allowing them to live out from under the control of their fathers or husbands. In their desire to be like other people, Christians retreated from the practice of equality between men and women and took refuge in the social conventions of their time. By the end of the first century, when the gospels were being written, the church had set aside the vision of Jesus in favor of a brotherhood that assigned to women their usual subservient role. Somewhere along the way the church lost sight of this new possibility, but with a little digging into the gospels we can uncover the evidence that points to Jesus's vision of a community comprised of sisters and brothers living and working as equals.

A Family of Equals

The gospel accounts in which Jesus declares that he has found a new family in the company of his followers demonstrate how easily the feminine can be lost when the exact meaning of Greek word *adelphoi*, "from the same womb," is unclear from the context:

> While he was still speaking to the crowds, his mother and his *adelphoi* were standing outside, wanting to speak to him. Someone told him, "Look, your mother and your *adelphoi* are standing outside, wanting to speak to you." But to the one who had told him this, Jesus replied, "Who is my mother, and who are my *adelphoi?*" And pointing to his disciples, he said, "Here are my mother and my *adelphoi*! For whoever does the will of my Father in heaven is my *adelphos* and *adelphe* and mother."[1]

Notice that *adelphoi*, which is usually translated "brothers" the four times it occurs in this brief passage, is sexually ambiguous. You cannot tell from the context if the mother of Jesus was accompanied by just her sons or by her daughters as well. The emphatic words attributed to Jesus, however, clear up any ambiguity, at least in the mind of the person who wrote this passage, about the way Jesus described his disciples. Those who did the will of the Father were both brothers and sisters to him.

Notice also that in this picture of the new family, all the members of the household are equals. No patriarch or *pater familias* presides over the family. The sisters and the brothers are all at the same level of authority. The only father mentioned is "in heaven." According to Matthew, Jesus hammered away at this theme of equality in the new family:

> But you are not to be called rabbi, for you have one teacher, and you are all *adelphoi*. And call no one your father on earth, for you have one Father—the one in heaven. Nor are you to be called instructors, for you have one instructor, the Messiah. The greatest among you will be your servant.[2]

Apparently many people who think of themselves as followers of Jesus have decided that Matthew misunderstood Jesus, since in many Christian communities we find people who insist on being called "Father" or some equivalent of rabbi or instructor. Pastor, reverend, and priest are all titles that people use to set themselves apart from the rest of the community in order to claim special wisdom and authority. The delight in titles is not restricted to those who hold them. Many members of Christian communities seem to like having someone special in charge of their spiritual lives. If Matthew was correct, however, in his assessment of the position taken by Jesus in regard to titles, many people may have entirely missed the point Jesus was making about the nature of the community he envisioned for his followers: a family of sisters and brothers with a father in heaven.

Instead of seeking status through titles, the sisters and brothers of Jesus are to accept the role of a servant—*diakonos* in the Greek of the New Testament. Apparently, some who followed Jesus found this idea of equality hard to take. They wanted to have positions of honor and power in what they imagined would be the new order in the realm Jesus would establish. Jesus harshly denounced such ambitions:

> "You know that the rulers of the Gentiles lord it over them, and their great ones are tyrants over them. It will not be so among you; but whoever wishes to be great among you must be your servant, and whoever wishes to be first among you must be your slave; just as the Son of Man came not to be served but to serve, and to give his life a ransom for many."[3]

According to Matthew, Jesus spoke plainly about what the servants were to do. In describing the work of the servants, Jesus at the same time expanded the circle of those he considered to be his sisters and brothers. These pronouncements come to us in the form of a parable. Jesus pictured a king inviting the righteous of the world into his kingdom, while the rest would be sent off to join "the devil and his angels." In the parable, both the righteous and the condemned express surprise that they had been tested without realizing that the test was in progress:

> "Then the righteous will answer him, 'Lord, when was it that we saw you hungry and gave you food, or thirsty and gave you something to drink? And when was it that we saw you a stranger and welcomed you, or naked and gave you clothing? And when was it that we saw you sick or in prison and visited you?' And the king will answer them, 'Truly I tell you, just as you did it to one of the least of these my *adelphoi*, you did it to me.'"[4]

If this passage accurately reflects what Jesus taught, he did not want his followers to limit their concern to their brothers and sisters in the new community but wanted them to take responsibility for any person in need. Anyone who is hungry or thirsty or in trouble is one of Jesus's brothers and sisters. The further we read in the gospels, the more radical the notion of the new family seems to be. It is one thing for a small community of like-minded people to see themselves as the family of Jesus, but quite another for them to think of social outcasts, as well as sick and hungry strangers, as their sisters and brothers.

In trying to figure out more precisely what Jesus had in mind for the way his followers were to treat one another and the people around them, we may be safe in assuming that he drew on family imagery from four sources: his observations of other people's families, the family into which he was born, his experience of his followers as his new family, and his reading of Hebrew Scripture. We are devoting the next chapter to the family imagery in the Hebrew Scriptures, but the other three sources deserve at least some attention.

The Trap of Family Loyalty

If Jesus ever had a positive thing to say about life in the families he observed, nobody bothered to preserve his remarks. On the contrary, he is reported to have urged his followers to break away from their families as he had done. In describing how Jesus attempted to train his followers to carry on the work he had begun, Matthew's gospel puts the teaching of Jesus about families this way:

> "I have come to set a man against his father, and a daughter against her mother, and a daughter-in-law against her mother-in-law; and one's foes will be members of one's own household. Whoever loves father or mother more than me is not worthy of me; and whoever loves son or daughter more than me is not worthy of me."[5]

According to Luke, Jesus had been even more emphatic: "Whoever comes to me and does not hate father and mother, wife and children, brothers and sisters, yes, and even life itself, cannot be my disciple."[6] We might wonder what Jesus had seen in first-century Palestinian family life that made him urge his followers to hate their parents, their sisters and brothers, their spouses, and even their own children. Those are strong words, ascribed to Jesus without explanation, but Matthew and Luke may have pro-

vided a clue in recounting a brief exchange between Jesus
and someone who seemed to have had a good excuse for
not dropping everything to follow him:

> Another of his disciples said to him, "Lord, first let me
> go and bury my father." But Jesus said to him, "Follow
> me, and let the dead bury their own dead."[7]

Anyone not acquainted with the customs of the region
in which Jesus lived and taught might think that he was
being unduly harsh. To our ears, it sounds as if someone
who wanted to follow Jesus had left his father's corpse
laid out in the front room and was asking for just enough
time to take care of the burial, certainly a reasonable request. In all probability, however, Luke and Matthew intended the story to convey the strong sense of family
loyalty that kept children bound to their parents until their
parents died. The disciple in the story was asking permission to delay a break with the family until the father's
death and the burial that would end the filial obligation.[8]

As Luke and Matthew understood Jesus's teaching,
those who stay bound to their parents until their parents
die are themselves "dead." They have no life of their own.
Their sense of identity, meaning, and purpose are derived
from their place in the family. Their family is their religion.
Their parents are filling a place in their lives that belongs
to God alone. Jesus had apparently observed that family
loyalty, which appeared to be a virtue, was in reality an
obstacle to developing confidence in God.

Jesus's Family of Origin

Perhaps Jesus found that his own family was as stifling
as the other families that he had observed. The gospels,
however, have precious little to say about the family in
which Jesus grew up. All four gospels pass along traditions
about Jesus and his mother and siblings, but only Matthew
and Luke try to fill in some of the blanks about his early
life with delightful stories about the birth and infancy of
Jesus. Although these stories have provided a jumping-off
place for endless speculations about the home life of the

young boy Jesus, the two gospels differ so much in detail that they do not offer a very coherent picture of the way Jesus's family was remembered by the early Christians. Matthew and Mark, however, show some agreement about the family of Jesus. Perhaps they present assumptions commonly held by Christians in the latter part of the first century. This is the way Matthew writes about the tradition:

> He came to his hometown and began to teach the people in their synagogue, so that they were astounded and said, "Where did this man get this wisdom and these deeds of power? Is not this the carpenter's son? Is not his mother called Mary? And are not his brothers James and Joseph and Simon and Judas? And are not all his sisters with us? Where then did this man get all this?"[9]

In telling the story about how little regard the people of Nazareth had for the teaching of the young man who had grown up in their midst, both Mark and Matthew mention the family profession. In Matthew the townspeople identify Jesus as a son of a *tekton*, while in Mark, Jesus himself is called a *tekton*. Most English-speaking Christians are accustomed to thinking of both Jesus and Joseph working in their little carpenter's shop to turn out simple products such as ox yokes, but in reality *tekton* was a term applied to all sorts of craftsmen. Joseph and his sons could have been shipbuilders or sculptors. They could have been engaged in making household furniture or in building houses.[10]

Noting that our English word "architect" evolved directly from this Greek word *tekton*, we have a possible clue about the nature of Jesus's home life. Craftsmen in the first century, like builders today, traveled widely from city to city, settling temporarily wherever they found work. Sometimes a craftsman would take his family along, and sometimes he would leave them behind in his home village. If this tradition of the family business has any validity, Jesus at one time or another may have lived for extended periods in a household without a father and at other times he may have known the sense of instability often experienced by children who are constantly up-rooted. It is quite possible that when Jesus was young and the family was small, the whole family went along wherever Joseph found work. It is also possible that a growing family would have made such an itinerant life impractical, so Joseph might have left them all in Nazareth. Then as each boy became old enough and skilled enough, Joseph might have taken him along.

Early Christian tradition suggests that after Jesus's death, at least some members of this good-sized family became part of the community that carried on his teaching. According to the Acts of the Apostles, "Mary the mother of Jesus, as well as his *adelphoi*" joined the little company of people that gathered in Jerusalem after Jesus was gone.[11] From the context it is impossible to tell whether the author meant to suggest that only the brothers of Jesus joined their mother Mary in Jerusalem or whether the statement means that their sisters came along as well. In all probability, however, Mary would have traveled with at least some of her daughters as well as her sons.

Apparently there is some confusion as to whether the third son born to Mary was named Joseph or Joses, and whether Judas or Simon was the youngest of the five boys, but that James took over the leadership of the Jerusalem church does not seem to have been a matter of dispute. The Acts of the Apostles says that soon after King Herod killed the disciple James, the brother of John, Jesus's younger brother James rose to a place of prominence in the Jerusalem church.[12] In writing to the Galatians, the apostle Paul showed unusual respect for "James the Lord's brother." Although the two of them were in fundamental disagreement about the importance to be given to Jewish law and custom in a Christian community with Gentile converts, Paul acknowledged James as an apostle, a designation he reserved for those people who took active leadership in spreading the message of Jesus Christ. Paul recognized only two members of the Jerusalem church as apostles: Peter and the Lord's brother, James.[13]

Writing in the fourth century, Eusebius the Bishop of Caesarea passed along another tradition about one of Jesus's younger brothers. He reports that the brother of Jesus whose name was Judas, sometimes called Jude to differentiate him from the traitor with the same name, had two grandsons who were revered as descendants of King David. Fearing the emergence of a dynastic tradition that might threaten his authority, the Emperor Domitian ordered the arrest of the two men, but when he discovered that they were merely poor farmers, he let them go.

That Jesus's younger brothers at first resisted his leadership but later became active participants in the church should not be surprising. Often the oldest child bears a heavy responsibility in the family, especially when one of the parents is frequently absent. With this responsibility often goes authority over the younger children. It is not hard to imagine the eldest son resenting the responsibility and the younger brothers and sisters resenting his authority. A younger brother as capable as James proved to be could easily have been so caught up in sibling rivalry that he could not appreciate the special mission Jesus had undertaken until after Jesus was dead.

The Lost Sister

So Jesus had four brothers remembered by name, two of whom left their marks on the record of the early church. But what about Jesus's sisters? What impact did they have on the development of their oldest brother's understanding of family? What parts did they play in the emerging church? Did Jesus have a younger sister? For many women that question arises from something more than academic curiosity. Sensitive to the masculine imagery Christians tend to use when speaking of God, these women feel shut out when the church offers Jesus as the sole example to be imitated. A contemporary songwriter, Dory Previn, picked up those feelings of rejection and longing in a song she wrote back in the early seventies. She has expressed those feelings of hurt with so much clarity and poignancy that men, too, can begin to under-

stand the limitations of a religion that has suppressed feminine imagery:

> did jesus have a baby sister?
> was she bitter?
> was she sweet?
> did she wind up in a convent?
> did she end up on the street?
> on the run?
> on the stage?
> did she dance?
> did he have a sister?
> a little baby sister?
> did jesus have a sister?
> did they give her a chance?
>
> did he have a baby sister?
> could she speak out
> by and large?
> or was she told by mother mary
> ask your brother he's in charge
> he's the chief
> he's the whipped cream
> on the cake
> did he have a sister?
> a little baby sister?
> did jesus have a sister?
> did they give her a break?
>
> her brother's
> birth announcement
> was pretty big
> pretty big
> i guess
> while she got precious
> little notice
> in the local press
> her mother was the virgin
> when she carried him

carried him
therein
if the little girl came later
then
was she conceived in sin?
and in sorrow?
and in suffering?
and in shame?
did jesus have a sister?
what was her name?

did she long to be the saviour
saving everyone
she met?
and in private to her mirror
did she whisper
saviourette?
saviourwoman?
saviourperson?
save your breath!
did he have a sister?
a little baby sister?
did jesus have a sister?
was she there at his death?

and did she cry for mary's comfort
as she watched him
on the cross?
and was mary too despairing
ask your brother
he's the boss
he's the chief
he's the man
he's the show
did he have a sister?
a little baby sister?
did jesus have a sister?
doesn't anyone know?

Looking back over what little the early Christians had to say about the family into which Jesus was born, we may be safe in making two assumptions that are critical in our understanding of what Jesus had in mind when he said that those who do the will of the father in heaven are his brothers and sisters. The association Jesus had with his younger sisters and brothers was sufficiently positive for him to decide on the family as a metaphor to use in his description of the ideal community, but his experience of his own family was sufficiently troubling for Jesus to imagine another kind of family: a family with a dependable father, a family in which each sister and brother could claim an equal share of authority.

The Lost "Sisters" of Jesus

The documents produced by the early church contain no specific recollections about the relationship of Jesus to his natural sisters, but all four gospels convey a tradition that Jesus was close to a number of women in his new family. Although the authors of the gospels were more interested in the men who followed Jesus than they were in the women, the memory of Jesus's unconventional dealings with his "sisters" was apparently too strong for them to ignore completely. Evidence of the importance of women to Jesus is scattered throughout the gospels.

The gospels also contain clues that suggest why women were attracted to Jesus. Dorothy Sayers—theologian, classics scholar, and author of mystery stories—has followed the clues and arrived at valuable conclusions:

> Perhaps it is no wonder that the women were first at the Cradle and last at the Cross. They had never known a man like this Man—and there has never been another. A prophet and teacher who never nagged at them, never flattered or coaxed or patronized; who never made jokes about them, never treated them either as "The women, God help us!" or "The ladies, God bless them!"; who rebuked without querulousness and praised without condescension; who took their questions and arguments

seriously; who never mapped out their sphere for them, never urged them to be feminine or jeered at them for being female; who had no axe to grind and no uneasy male dignity to defend; who took them as he found them and was completely unself-conscious. There is no act, no sermon, no parable in the whole Gospel that borrows its pungency from female perversity; nobody could possibly guess from the words and deeds of Jesus that there was anything "funny" about woman's nature.[14]

The prominent place of women among the friends of Jesus comes through most clearly near the end of the gospels. Although the gospels differ on the details, they agree that a number of women who had followed Jesus from Galilee were present at his execution and that women were the first to discover the empty tomb. All of the gospels say it was the women who informed the men that the tomb could not hold the Jesus they had known and loved.

Unlike the "daughters of Jerusalem," who beat their breasts and wailed at the sight of Jesus being taken away for crucifixion, the women from Galilee were silent. The Jerusalem women had not known Jesus so well or for so long a time as his friends from Galilee. According to the gospels, the women who had been with Jesus from the beginning of his ministry betrayed emotion only when they discovered that his tomb was empty. The gospels say that they were afraid, alarmed, terrified. What did they have to fear? Perhaps they understood the terrible cost of the responsibility they had been given to carry on the work Jesus had begun. Perhaps they understood the repeated call of Jesus to follow him. Perhaps they had a glimpse of the enormity of the task they faced because they understood Jesus better than either the male disciples or the women who had flocked to him in the last days.

Matthew and Mark say that these women who were with Jesus at the end had followed him and provided for him when he was in Galilee.[15] The word "provide" translates the Greek *diakoneo,* which can mean wait on, serve, care for, look after, or help. It is the verb form of *diak-*

onos, the word usually translated "servant," that described the role that Jesus had in mind for all his brothers and sisters. The designation "deacon" evolved from the same root. In the early church the people called deacons were those whose saw to it that all the members of the community were fed and cared for.

We must not suppose, however, that the people in the early church who were remembered for their faithfulness in the servant role were limited to providing food and drink for those with more important assignments. Stephen, first introduced in the Acts of the Apostles as one of the Hellenists appointed to wait on tables, was killed for proclaiming the message of Christ. The call to follow is a call to take up the cross, to confront the kingdoms of the world with a new possibility for human life, to call Jesus and not Caesar "Lord."

Further on in Acts, we read about two men who are described with the same word, *diakoneo*, that was used for the women who looked after Jesus. Paul was sending Timothy and Erastus to Macedonia with something more to do than to cook and clean; he was entrusting them with an important mission. When Paul writes of his own work, he frequently uses the same kind of language, describing himself as a servant (*diakonos*) and his responsibility as ministry (*diakonia*).[16]

By the time the gospels were written, *diakoneo* and all its related forms had taken on special meaning in the church. Surely the use of this word to describe the women who were closest to Jesus could be no accident. These women understood and practiced what Jesus taught about serving other people, but they must have done much more. If those who bore the designation after them were also known as teachers and apostles, the "sisters" of Jesus must have been teachers and leaders as well. These women showed subsequent generations what Jesus meant when he called on his followers to be sisters and brothers.

The women who were the closest friends of Jesus during his life must have been a guiding influence in the community that survived his death. The Acts of the Apostles hints as much when it names the eleven men from the inner circle who chose to stay together after Jesus's departure. The account goes on to say that they were constantly devoting themselves to prayer, "together with certain women."[17] The women must have been those identified in the gospels as the ones who stayed with Jesus at the cross.

While Jesus was still alive, these women began their decisive role in the community. The gospels do not dwell on such mundane questions as, How did Jesus and his disciples survive on their itinerant ministry? How did they eat? What did they do for money? The only clue is the mention of the women providers. Although Matthew and Mark do not describe the women in this way until near the end of their stories, Luke makes a point of it when he describes the tour Jesus made through Galilee:

> Soon afterwards he went on through cities and villages, proclaiming and bringing the good news of the kingdom of God. The twelve were with him, as well as some women who had been cured of evil spirits and infirmities: Mary, called Magdalene, from whom seven demons had gone out, and Joanna, the wife of Herod's steward Chuza, and Susanna, and many others, who provided for them out of their resources.[18]

In describing the women who were among Jesus's closest associates, however, Luke has betrays his failure to grasp the full implications of the community of equals Jesus had envisioned for his followers. Although he never mentions any prior illnesses of the men who were in the entourage of Jesus, Luke makes a point of telling his readers that the women who were most generous in their financial support of Jesus's ministry had been sick or "infirm." In spite of Luke's condescending description of the women, however, one inescapable fact emerges. Jesus received his financial backing primarily from women, who were his partners in ministry.

Another example of Luke's habit of treating women differently than men is evident in his story of Joanna. She is identified chiefly by the name and position of her hus-

band—"Joanna, the wife of Herod's steward Chuza"—as if
she had no importance in her own right. Yet the next we
hear of her is in Luke's account of the crucifixion, death,
burial, and resurrection of Jesus:

> When all the crowds who had gathered there for this
> spectacle saw what had taken place, they returned
> home, beating their breasts. But all his acquaintances, in-
> cluding the women who had followed him from Galilee,
> stood at a distance, watching these things.[19]

After Luke tells of Joseph of Arimathea's receiving the
body of Jesus from Pilate and laying it in a new tomb, his
account of the women continues:

> It was the day of Preparation, and the sabbath was be-
> ginning. The women who had come with him from Gali-
> lee followed, and they saw the tomb, and how his body
> was laid. Then they returned, and prepared spices and
> ointments.
>
> On the sabbath they rested according to the command-
> ment.
>
> But on the first day of the week, at early dawn, they
> came to the tomb, taking the spices they had prepared.

The women found the tomb empty, and they heard the
word of Jesus's resurrection from the angel guard, and
they remembered his word that on the third day he would
rise. Returning from the tomb, "they told all this to the
eleven and to all the rest. Now it was Mary Magdalene, and
Joanna, Mary the mother of James, and the other women
with them who told this to the apostles."[20]

What occurred in Joanna's life between the time she
was healed of infirmities and when she risked life and limb
to participate in performing the last sacred rites for a condemned criminal? She was the wife of a high official in
Herod's court, a profligate court where all kinds of scan-
dals took place, such as the beheading of John the Baptist.
Is that what caused her "infirmities?" Did Jesus heal her,
mind and body and soul? Did she leave all and follow him?

Such speculations about a woman mentioned in a gospel narrative can upset Christians in a way that speculations about men do not. If they are willing to imagine anything at all about Joanna, they might prefer to picture her staying in her marriage and retaining her position in Herod's court. They do not find it easy to entertain the idea that a woman might have made an independent decision to abandon her family and her life among the officials of the ruling class and used her own money to support the ministry of Jesus.

Yet Joanna's place in the story encourages the reader to wonder how women responded to the radical message Jesus was proclaiming: "Whoever comes to me and does not hate father and mother, wife and children, brothers and sisters, yes, and even life itself, cannot be my disciple." Did Joanna truly understand the new community he was calling into being? What a threat her story would have been to the community one generation after the resurrection, when the young church was trying to establish itself as a model household upholding all the conservative standards Jesus had challenged. Maybe it was just as well to play down this woman who had taken him so seriously.

Although Luke's gospel is generally regarded as sympathetic to women, he is no different from the other gospels in playing down their contributions. Unlike Matthew and John, Luke does not even include an appearance of the risen Lord to a woman. Luke's silence on the subject of the women whom Jesus accepted as sisters may be the reason why many women today do not regard Luke as an author who was concerned about them.

The part played by Joanna has been submerged, but the woman identified as Susanna has almost disappeared completely. She does not appear again in any of the gospels. Only Mary Magdalene is a central character in the story retold by the first Christians as they recalled the events preceding and following the death of Jesus. She is the only person unambiguously named in all four gospels as being present at the death of Jesus and at the empty tomb. She was the first person to whom the risen Lord appeared and gave the apostolic commission, "Go...and tell."[21] Despite the evidence that Mary Magdalene was the first person appointed to be an apostle of the risen Lord, Christians over the centuries have identified her with the unnamed women in the story and confused her with others named Mary. All we can say about her with any accuracy is that she was remembered in the early church as the first person who demonstrated confidence in Jesus after his death.

Of the other women who provided for Jesus, the gospels provide at least two with some identification. The community remembered them as mothers of his disciples. Matthew, Mark, and Luke identify one of the mothers as another Mary who was with Mary Magdalene at the crucifixion and at the tomb. She is variously described as the mother of James and Joseph, the mother of James the younger and of Joses, and by implication as the mother of James. What seems likely is that this Mary was also well known in the early Christian community. One of her sons was James, listed with the twelve disciples as the son of Alphaeus.[22] He was also called James the *mikros*—which could have meant younger, but might also have meant shorter or less important—to distinguish him from James the brother of John and from James the brother of Jesus. Another son, called Joseph or Joses, probably joined the Christian community later.

Matthew alone includes a second mother at the crucifixion, "the mother of the sons of Zebedee," but he fails to provide her with a name.

Only one other woman is named in the gospels as one of those who looked after Jesus. Mark calls her Salome and says that she was with the two Marys at the crucifixion and at the empty tomb. She needed no other identification because in the corporate memory of the church she had a place that did not depend on the reputation of a son or of anyone else.

What conclusions can we draw about Jesus's vision of a new family from his dealings with the women mentioned in the gospels as those who financed his work, traveled with him, and looked after him and his disciples? Some parts of the picture seem to come into focus when we look at the importance of these women who became sisters of Jesus.

The women who looked after Jesus were far more than providers of food and money. They were the prototypes of all those later followers of Jesus who described themselves as servants—the same terms the gospel writers used in identifying the women. In wisdom, faith, and courage they were more than the equals of their brothers in the new family.

Jesus was not ashamed to accept help and sustenance from his women friends. As he willingly gave of himself to teach and heal them, he willingly received their gifts to him.

The sisters of Jesus were not confined to any age group. He counted among the members of his new family both women his own age and women of his mother's generation.

The women had a better grasp of what Jesus was trying to teach them than the men, and had more courage to face the implications of that teaching. When his new brothers deserted him, his new sisters stayed with him, enduring the shame of the cross in their determination to give him an honorable burial.

The sisters of Jesus then confronted the timorous and discouraged men with the possibility of a new life for them all as the risen body of Christ. The women had discovered that their experience of Jesus was not to end with his death. In spite of their tendency to downplay the role of women, the gospel writers could not totally obscure the tradition that the women first glimpsed the reality of Jesus living on in the community he had gathered.

Respect for Troubled Sisters

According to Luke, some of the women whom Jesus healed became part of his entourage, but many others apparently accepted his help with thanks and went on their various ways. Although their stories were told, and retold, and were no doubt improved upon with each telling, their names were forgotten. What the people who formed the early church did remember, however, was the respect Jesus showed these troubled women:

> Then suddenly a woman who had been suffering from hemorrhages for twelve years came up behind him and touched the fringe of his cloak, for she said to herself, "If I only touch his cloak, I will be made well." Jesus turned, and seeing her he said, "Take heart, daughter; your faith has made you well." And instantly the woman was made well.[23]

To see this account as simply a miracle tale is to miss the point. This timid woman suffered from an illness that made her ritually unclean to her family and neighbors. She not only suffered from the loss of blood, but also from the loss of her place in the community. When she reached out to Jesus, she had every reason to expect that he would pull away in disgust like everyone else. Instead he addressed her warmly, as if she were a younger member of his own family, offered her encouragement, and assured her that she was a person of faith.

Jesus had such respect for women that the gospels even preserve a story about the time when he allowed a woman, and a foreigner at that, to teach him a lesson:

> Jesus left that place and went away to the district of Tyre and Sidon. Just then a Canaanite woman from that region came out and started shouting, "Have mercy on me, Lord, Son of David; my daughter is tormented by a demon." But he did not answer her at all. And his disciples came and urged him, saying, "Send her away, for she keeps shouting after us." He answered, "I was sent only to the lost sheep of the house of Israel." But she came and knelt before him, saying, "Lord, help me." He answered, "It is not fair to take the children's food and throw it to the dogs." She said, "Yes, Lord, yet even the dogs eat the crumbs that fall from their masters' table." Then Jesus answered her, "Woman, great is your faith!

Let it be done for you as you wish." And her daughter
was healed instantly.[24]

Jesus was exhausted, not just from the exertions of public speaking but from the demands people placed upon
him. As many harassed and tired people do today, he
sought a quiet place to rest in a village by the sea, a place
where no one would recognize him. He had no sooner arrived than one of the local women started shouting at him
to help her daughter. He tried to handle her by pretending
that she did not exist, but his disciples observed that this
tactic was not working and urged him to take action to get
rid of her. So Jesus told her clearly that he had no interest
in talking with foreigners; his only responsibility was for
his own people. When she persisted with her demands for
help, he tried to dismiss her with a racist epithet of the
sort that Jews frequently used when talking about their Ca-
naanite neighbors. Taking time for people like her would
be like taking bread from hungry children and throwing it
to dogs.

Instead of retreating in humiliation and anger, the Ca-
naanite woman held her ground. She took the nasty anal-
ogy that Jesus had used, twisted it around, and threw it
back at him. Even the dogs get the crumbs that fall from
the table, she told him, and that remark seems to have broken through Jesus's defenses. He no longer saw her as an
annoying foreign pest but as a human being of great faith.
He acknowledged the legitimacy of her claim on him, and
her daughter was healed. She stood up to him as a sister
would to her brother, and he finally responded to her with
the respect a brother owes his sister.

Mary and Martha

The way Jesus treated women provided the model for
what he meant by brother and sister. It did not take long
for the church to confuse and distort the model, but we
can spend some time with it and explore some of its new
possibilities for ourselves. The brother and sister relation-

ship between Jesus and Mary and Martha is good to examine because the story is so well known and so distorted.[25]

Mary Cartledge-Hayes, a feminist with a traditional biblical stance, has written a book, *To Love Delilah*, about "women your Sunday school teacher told you were irredeemable." She begins each essay with what she calls "popular wisdom." The "popular wisdom" about Martha goes:

> Mary and Jesus were having an absolutely fascinating conversation about God. Martha was stomping around banging clay pots together and muttering under her breath. Suddenly her bad temper got the best of her. "Mary!" she yelled. "Get in here and help me!" "Why, Martha," said Jesus, "I'm surprised at you! What Mary is doing is important; what you are doing isn't."
>
> And the moral of the story is: Whatever women do is wrong.[26]

What is the biblical background for this popular point of view? The story of the sisters occurs in three passages: the well-known story in the Gospel of Luke, a less well-known one in the Gospel of John, and a second, very muddled version by John of what must have been a powerful tradition in the early church.

As Luke tells it:

> Now as they went on their way, he entered a certain village, where a woman named Martha welcomed him into her home. She had a sister named Mary, who sat at the Lord's feet and listened to what he was saying. But Martha was distracted by her many tasks (*diakonia*); so she came to him and asked, "Lord, do you not care that my sister has left me to do all the work (*diakoneo*) by myself? Tell her then to help me." But the Lord answered her, "Martha, Martha, you are worried and distracted by many things; there is need of only one thing. Mary has chosen the better part, which will not be taken away from her."[27]

Mary and Martha were two sisters who had a home in a quiet little village very close to Jerusalem. It was a haven for Jesus. There a weary teacher found rest and the companionship of two women who cared for him and for whom he cared.

They were very different types of women. Martha, who was probably the older—the house is described as her home—was energetic and competent. Mary was quiet, eager for new ideas. Jesus enjoyed the company of both women, and both of the sisters loved this man who had upset their serene lives with his urgent message that suggested the approach of a turning point in history.

Mary could not hear enough about it. Martha wanted to hear about it, too, but she thought there were other things to be done. Her plan was that if the two of them worked together to get the dinner on the table, soon they both could hear all that Jesus had to say. So sure was she of the reasonableness of her plan that she enlisted Jesus's help. Jesus knew Martha well. He respected her as a leader and manager much like himself, and he recognized the legitimacy of her complaint, but he also knew the futility of trying to intervene in an argument between two sisters. A person with his sensitivity to human dynamics was not going to convey messages between two people in the same room and set up the kind of family triangle that inevitably leads to misunderstanding and misery. Jesus also recognized that Martha's concerns were different from those of her sister. He said, "Martha, Martha, you are worried and distracted by many things. There is need of only one thing. Mary has chosen the better part, which will not be taken away from her."

Whole theologies have been built on this verse, interpreting the"one thing" to be everything from "Jesus didn't need a lot of food" to "Mary is the model for the only life acceptable to Jesus."

Far from telling Martha to be like Mary, as the most egregious of the commentators on this passage have it, Jesus assured Martha she was all right just as she was. A better translation of "worried and distracted" would make

Jesus's affirmation of Martha more clear. A more literal interpretation would have Jesus say not that Martha was worried by many things, but that she had many things to take care of and much to be concerned about. To have Jesus call Martha "distracted" sounds like a rebuke, but the Greek word suggests instead that she was kept off balance by the constant demands other people were placing on her and her constant desire to respond. If she needed one thing, that was to be more centered so that she might better keep her balance in the midst of conflicting pressures. In the language Luke used, Jesus told Martha that he understood the weight of the responsibility she had shouldered and appreciated the gifts she demonstrated in taking on the burden of her many tasks.

The "better part" that Mary had chosen was the affirmation of her choice. The better part was not what she chose, but her commitment to her choice. Jesus was telling Martha she needed to recognize that her gifts were different from her sister's and equally valuable. Their heavenly Father's household could accommodate people with a variety of talents and could use all of their contributions.

This conjecture is borne out by the next memory of the sisters, which was kept by the Johannine community.[28] Their brother Lazarus had been stricken with a serious illness, and the sisters had sent to Jesus for help. After a long Johannine dialogue about the purpose of the illness, finally Jesus leaves for Bethany. Before he gets there Lazarus dies, and when he arrives Lazarus has already been buried and a wake is in progress. When Martha hears that Jesus is coming, she goes to meet him—the same Martha we know. Picture the scene: Martha in all her grief, giving Jesus a piece of her mind.

"If you had come when I told you to, my brother would not have died."

"Calm down, Martha, your brother will rise again."

"I know he will rise in the resurrection on the last day," she replied.

So much for those who think, "This woman knew only about pots and pans!" But there is even more. John, the much-loved spiritual evangelist, has Jesus make to Martha one of the great "I Am" statements in the gospel by which Jesus reveals who he is. "I am the Resurrection," he tells her. "Do you believe this?" And she replies in the words that Matthew, Mark, and Luke attribute to Peter and on which the Roman Catholic Church established its priority as Peter's successor. Martha the manager says, "Yes, Lord, I believe that you are the Messiah, the Christ." She takes her place beside the apostle as being one of the only two people in the New Testament record who recognized Jesus of Nazareth as the Messiah before the resurrection. The brother, who did not demand that insight always be packaged in the same way, called forth the statement of faith from her.

After offering the splendid picture of a woman recognizing God's presence in Jesus of Nazareth, John then proceeds to sully the memory of that woman's sister. After Martha's high moment, he inserts a story about Mary anointing Jesus's feet. One way of testing the authenticity of an event in the life of Jesus is by seeing how many evangelists tell the story. Only Palm Sunday, the crucifixion, and the resurrection appear in all four gospels—and one other story, the story of a woman anointing Jesus.

In the Gospel of Mark, just before the Last Supper, Jesus is at the home of Simon the Leper in Bethany.[29] While Jesus is at the table a woman comes with a jar of costly ointment and pours the ointment *on his head*. The men who were present expressed indignation that such expensive ointment had been wasted in this way; it should have been sold and the proceeds given to the poor. But Jesus defended her and said that she had anointed his body beforehand, for burial, and wherever his story was told, what she had done would be told in memory of her. She anointed his head, proclaiming him a king. Did she see him as a king who would die? Did she understand the nature of his kingship? Or is the radical Gospel of Mark telling the story of a rebel group who was sending a message to Jesus that there was an army out there ready to proclaim him king and do battle to support that claim?[30]

The Gospel of Matthew keeps the story essentially as Mark tells it. The time is Passover, and a woman pours the ointment on his head. Men object—the disciples this time—and Jesus defends her with the same words, saying that wherever his story is heard, what she has done will be told in memory of her. Luke alters many of the details and uses the story to illustrate a parable about the response to forgiveness. As is his custom, Luke presents the woman in a subservient role, but this time the woman is a sinner. She is weeping and bathes the feet of Jesus with her tears and wipes them with her hair, and then she kisses his feet and anoints them. When the host, a Pharisee, is offended that Jesus let a sinner touch him, Jesus tells the parable of two debtors who are forgiven their debts, one for a small sum and the other for a large one. He asks the Pharisee which one will love the creditor more. The Pharisee responds, "The one for whom the greater debt was canceled." Luke has Jesus contrast the gracious behavior of the woman who knew she was a sinner with the ungracious response of the Pharisee who had no sense of sin.

Finally, the evangelist John used the story for his own purposes. John has just recorded Martha's apostolic insight: "I believe that you are the Christ." Then he takes the name of her sister Mary, the eager learner, the forerunner of the women rabbis, and gives it to the nameless sinful woman in Luke's story. By casting her in the role of the woman with the ointment, John made it possible for tradition to confuse Mary of Bethany with another woman named Mary, Mary Magdalene, whose name was also attached to the stories about the nameless sinner who anointed Jesus. For those who have not taken the trouble to sort out the confusion, Mary Magdalene—the first person to whom the risen Lord appeared—continues to be the tainted sister of Martha.

Once we unscramble the traditions about Mary and Martha, the relationship of Jesus to these women gives us a glimpse into the way Jesus understood his mission. It may be that Jesus of Nazareth saw himself as the firstborn of many brothers for the new possibility that he called the kingdom of God. He envisioned a way of life for men and women working and growing together, a way that was radically different from what his people, and all the peoples of the world, lived out. Jesus was the new reality in the world. Truly, there had never been a man like him, but he saw himself as beginning a community that would live out his vision to the ends of the earth.

That community was the new family, the unexplored relationship of brother and sister: a supportive, caring, challenging relationship that was rooted and grounded in the new belonging—"the will of the Father"—and in no way a threat to any other relationship of men and women in the community. In this new community, a man could have many sisters; a woman could have many brothers. Each would be unique. Mary could let the dinner burn while she explored and challenged all the ideas Jesus brought, and he would never tire of her active, searching mind. Martha could think that Mary's priorities were skewed (and Jesus's as well) and she could tell him so. Each could bring to their relationship the peculiar gifts each had. Each could know and value the particular gifts the others offered, and all could know they were in the service of God.

In his choice of the sister-brother metaphor for talking about relationships in the kingdom of God, Jesus in all probability drew on traditions found in the Hebrew Scriptures, as did Paul and those who carried on his work. In the next chapter we will turn to some Old Testament narratives about brothers and sisters. Just as those ancient tales may have illuminated the family imagery used by Jesus and his earliest followers, the stories may give us a better understanding of the possibilities Jesus had in mind for women and men trying to live and work together.

Endnotes

1. Matt. 12:46-50; see also Mark 3:31-35 and Luke 8:19-21.
2. Matt. 23:8-11.
3. Matt. 20:25-28.

4. Matt. 25:37-40.

5. Matt. 10:35-37; see also Luke 12:51-53.

6. Luke 14:26.

7. Matt. 8:21-22; see also Luke 9:59-60.

8. Kenneth E. Bailey, *Through Peasant Eyes* (Grand Rapids, MI: Eerdmans, 1980), pp. 25-27.

9. Matt. 13:54-56; see also Mark 6:1-6, where the brothers are listed as "James and Joses and Judas and Simon."

10. See the commentary on Matthew 13:55 by W. F. Albright and C. F. Mann in *Matthew*, The Anchor Bible (Garden City, NY: Doubleday, 1971).

11. Acts 1:14.

12. Acts 12:1-2, 17.

13. Gal. 1:19 and 2:7-8.

14. Dorothy L. Sayers, *Are Women Human?* (Grand Rapids, MI: Eerdmans, 1971), p. 47.

15. Matt. 27:55-56 and Mark 15:40-41.

16. Acts 19:22; see Rom. 11:13; 1 Cor. 3:5; 2 Cor. 6:3-4.

17. Acts 1:14.

18. Luke 8:1-3.

19. Luke 23:48-49.

20. Luke 23:54-24:10.

21. Matt. 28:7 and John 20:17.

22. Matt. 10:2-4, Mark 3:16-19, and Luke 6:14-16.

23. Matt. 9:20-22; see also Mark 5:25-34 and Luke 8:43-48.

24. Matt. 15:21-28; see also Mark 7:24-30.

25. Renita J. Weems, a Black "womanist," in her study of women's relationships in the Bible, *Just A Sister Away* (LuraMedia, 1988), has the two women rethink the incident in monologues in which each is finally able to affirm the value of what she has to offer without any need to disparage the other. In exploring this story, Weems sees a possibility that great scholars throughout the ages have missed. Elisabeth Moltmann-Wendel, in her scholarly tracings of the fortunes of the sisters throughout the ages, details the rise and fall of the two sisters, each age always choosing one ahead of the other. Martin Luther would have no work but the work of Mary, while Rudolf Bultmann thought Martha showed the true attitude of faith. Moltmann-Wendel also recounts the history of Martha's rise and Mary's fall during the middle ages.

26. Mary Cartledge-Hayes, *To Love Delilah* (LuraMedia, 1990), p. 67.

27. Luke 10:38-42.

28. John 11:17-35.

29. Mark 14:3-9; Matt. 26:6-13; Luke 7:36-50; John 12:1-8.

30. Ched Myers, *Binding the Strong Man: A Political Reading of Mark's Story of Jesus* (Maryknoll, NY: Orbis, 1988), p. 360.

Chapter 2

The Sister•Brother Stories in Hebrew Scripture

hen the first Christians learned that Jesus had envisioned a community made up of people who thought of themselves as sisters and brothers, their knowledge of the Hebrew Scriptures would have shaped their understanding of what Jesus had in mind. In all probability, their picture of what a brother and sister meant to each other was conditioned by ancient laws and customs as well as by their favorite stories about such well-remembered sisters as Rebekah, Miriam, Dinah, and Tamar.

As Jews, Jesus and his earliest followers would also have been familiar with the sacred writings of their people. When they were children, their mothers and grandmothers would have told them the stories that had gripped the imaginations of Hebrew-speaking people for centuries. Although by the time of Jesus Hebrew was no longer a spoken language, the stories continued to live in the vernacular, constantly refreshed by the learned people who read them aloud in the ancient tongue at synagogue and retold them in the language that the people could understand.

As Gentiles came into the Christian communities, they heard Greek translations of the stories that had guided the thinking of the Jewish people. In a short time the Gentile as well as the Jewish followers of Jesus used the images and metaphors of the Hebrew Scriptures to describe life in their new communities of faith. Following the example of Jesus, Greek-speaking Christians favored figures of speech that emerged from the ancient tradition. The stories about sisters and brothers provided them with a frame of reference as they worked out new ways for women and men to divide responsibility and authority in these communities.

Although most of the Hebrew Scriptures support a social structure dominated by men, the followers of Jesus had two kinds of biblical stories they could use to their advantage in challenging conventional family arrangements. One kind of story includes the tales of women who changed the course of history by their decisive acts of courage: Deborah and Jael, Naomi and Ruth, Esther, and Judith. The other kind focused on women who, at first glance, appear to play merely supportive roles in the biblical drama, such as Sarah, Rebekah, and Rachel. A closer reading, however, reveals that those who told the stories of these wives and sisters did so with admiration and respect for their subjects.

The appreciation of women demonstrated in some of the stories has led two literary scholars, Harold Bloom and David Rosenberg, to suggest that a woman wrote them. They think that this anonymous author, known as "J" because of the name these stories use for God, "Jahweh," was an aristocrat of King David's court. "The largest assumption of all writers on the Bible," writes Harold Bloom, "is that 'It is a theological work, as well as historical and literary.'" Bloom claims he can understand J because he is neither a believer nor a historian; nor, he contends, was J. "When script becomes Scripture," Bloom daringly states, "reading is numbed by a taboo and inhibition."[1]

Bloom identifies J as a woman because she had no heroes, only heroines. Sarah and Rachel are admirable; Abraham, Jacob, and Moses receive mixed treatment.[2] By portraying women in a more favorable light than men, J may have been attempting to promote a better balance in relationships between the sexes. The women in her stories are generally wiser than the men. They tend to see what is best for the family and the community, but they must often be devious in getting their way because of the oppressive nature of their patriarchal society. In many of J's stories, the shrewd women find ways of doing what they perceive to be the will of God. In doing what they have to do in order to fulfill what they see to be the destiny of their people, the women in J's stories fit the definition of the kind of people Jesus claimed for his new family: "Whoever does the will of my Father in heaven is my brother and sister."

For J, community and society are extensions of the relationships between husbands and wives, parents and children, brothers and sisters. Her sensitivity to the dynamics between men and women make her stories especially valuable for people trying to figure out appropriate ways for men and women to treat each other, and her stories encourage men to listen to women and to respect their wisdom. J also warns that if men use their superior size and physical strength to dominate women, women will find more subtle ways to exercise power. In telling her stories, J herself seems to be using a subtle method for putting forward the ideas that ultimately led Jesus to imagine the possibility of creating a society in which men and women regard each other as equals.

By challenging the assumption that only the writings of men, never women, could have found their way into the Bible, Bloom and Rosenberg have opened up important ways of thinking about our religious heritage. For centuries, Jews and Christians alike refused to entertain the idea that women might have contributed psalms and stories to the collection of holy writings, and this narrow approach to Scripture has endured in spite of the fact we know that in most societies women are the bearers of tradition and their gifts for poetry and song are equal to men's. Once we set aside the prejudices imposed by our culture, we can begin to wonder how many contributions of women writers have been ignored or attributed to men. If brothers and sisters are to be equal in the present, then we must discard our automatic assumption of male authorship when we approach any piece of literature from the past.

Rebekah, Laban, and Isaac

A sensitivity to women doing the will of God comes through most clearly in two kinds of brother-sister stories that feature Rebekah, the sister of Laban and wife of Isaac. These narratives show Rebekah cooperating with her brother Laban and manipulating her husband Isaac, who at one point in the story actually claims that Rebekah is his sister.

Rebekah was beautiful, considerate, and capable—an answer to Abraham's prayer that he might find among his own people a wife for his son Isaac. Abraham sent a servant back to the home he had left in Ur of the Chaldeans. As soon as the servant arrived at his destination, he was struck by the appearance of a graceful young woman who drew water from the well for him and for his camels. He introduced himself, offered her expensive presents, and inquired about her people.

As soon as her brother Laban heard about this emissary from Abraham, he rushed out to meet him, and immediately took charge of arranging hospitality. To further his sister's best interests, Laban unloaded the camels, provided straw and fodder for them, and brought water to the visitors so that they could wash their feet. Laban's enthusiastic welcome of Abraham's envoy may have been occasioned by the jewels with which the envoy adorned and charmed his sister Rebekah. Both the brother and the sister recognized the economic advantages of forming a marriage alliance with their relatives who had prospered by moving to the land of Canaan.

Laban was present and active during the negotiations concerning his sister's marriage to Isaac, but he may have been reluctant to see her leave. He joined their mother in asking, "Let the girl remain with us a while, at least ten days."[3] When Abraham's servant refused to delay, Laban and their mother called Rebekah and left the decision up to her: "Will you go with this man?" She said simply, "I

will." Laban bade his sister farewell, giving her his blessing, letting her go without any assurance that he would
ever hear from her again.

Rebekah married Isaac. After a long period of barren-
ness, in answer to prayer, she conceived twins—two very
different sons. The hairy, ruddy son who came first from
the womb was called Esau, or "ruffian," and the second
one who came clutching his brother's heel was called Jacob, or "heel-clutcher." Rebekah had given birth to sons
who were twins but who were of completely different
temperaments:

> When the boys grew up, Esau was a skillful hunter, a
> man of the field, while Jacob was a quiet man, living in
> tents. Isaac loved Esau, because he was fond of game;
> but Rebekah loved Jacob.[4]

Because Esau had been born first, according to custom
he should have replaced his father Isaac as patriarch of the
clan, but Rebekah saw that he lacked the wit and the wisdom to be a leader. He was an athletic oaf who lived for
the moment, unable to see the future implications of present actions. For example, one day when he came home
hungry from hunting, he readily agreed to hand his birth-
right over to his brother Jacob for a bowl of lentil soup.
Not surprisingly, Rebekah did not want to leave the destiny of her descendants in his incompetent hands. Her husband Isaac was either too dull-witted or too bound by
tradition to admit that their second son was better
equipped to lead than was Esau. Rebekah had to trick her
husband, now grown old and blind, into transferring his
authority to Jacob through a ritual blessing. Over Jacob's
objections, she dressed him in his brother's clothes, and
had him bring the meal that the old man expected from
his first-born son, pretending to be Esau in order to claim
the blessing.[5]

Naturally Esau was outraged when he learned that his
brother had tricked him out of the blessing that was right-
fully his. As do most men with more brawn than brains, he
decided to get even through violent means: "The days of

mourning for my father are approaching; then I will kill my brother Jacob." Rebekah heard about the threat so she called her younger son Jacob and warned him, "Your brother Esau is consoling himself by planning to kill you." She then insisted that Jacob flee at once to her brother Laban in Haran. She advised him to stay in Haran with Laban until Esau's anger cooled and he forgot what Jacob had done to him. She promised that when the time was right she would send for him.[6]

Although they may not have seen each other for many years, Rebekah could be confident that Laban would offer protection for her son. She knew she could count on Laban to welcome her son into the family she had left.

> When Laban heard the news about his sister's son Jacob, he ran to meet him; he embraced him and kissed him, and brought him to his house. Jacob told Laban all these things, and Laban said to him, "Surely you are my bone and my flesh!"[7]

As the story unfolds, however, the reader sees that Laban provided Jacob with something more than safety. He could offer the boy something that his mother could not. As the mother's favorite, Jacob was soft to the point of being spoiled, and preferred women's occupations to the work usually assigned to men. Rebekah needed her brother's help in making a man out of this bright, sensitive boy. Jacob spent twenty years working for his uncle. He married two of his uncle's daughters, and fathered children by them and their maids. He regularly matched wits with his uncle, sometimes winning and sometimes losing. He emerged from this prolonged experience a seasoned leader, prepared to wrestle with angels and to take over the leadership of his clan back home.

Together, Rebekah and her brother Laban had assured the future of the family Rebekah had mothered. To develop leadership ability, young people need the guidance of both strong men and strong women. The brother of Jacob's mother was able to give him what his father could not, an example of what it means to be a subtle but decisive head of a family. For the sake of the next generation, the sister-brother team had nurtured a leader, the mythic father of the twelve tribes of Israel.

When Christians incorporated the sister-brother metaphor into their self-understanding as a community, they were accepting mutual responsibility for their children. Over the ages, brothers and sisters have often collaborated in rearing their offspring. A mother bringing up her children in the city may send them off in the summer to work with her brother on the family farm. A father whose wife has died at an early age may feel overwhelmed by responsibility for several small children and ask his sister to take the youngest. In the Christian "family," parents could expect a similar kind of help and cooperation from many of their new sisters and brothers in the sometimes arduous task of child-rearing. Many communities until recent times taught children to recognize the "brothers" and "sisters" of their parents by telling them to call adults in the new family their "aunts" and "uncles." By extending the family metaphor to create a bridge between the generations, Christian communities encouraged children to respect and learn from a wider circle of adults than their natural families could provide. In many instances the aunts and uncles in the new family could make up for whatever positive influence was missing or weak in the natural parents.

The cooperation of Rebekah and Laban in preparing her son Jacob for leadership provided J with one aspect of the writer's skillful exploration of the complexities that typify interactions between men and women. J examined yet another aspect of the subject in the story of how Rebekah managed her husband, but oddly enough, J presents Rebekah not just as Isaac's wife but also as his sister.[8] Later we will turn our attention to the curious tales of the sister-wives, but here let us recall the wisdom Rebekah demonstrated in choosing Jacob over his brother Esau to lead the family. Isaac was so bound by tradition that he was blind to the failings of his older son. Rebekah saw that something more than masculine proficiency would be required for guiding the clan in the next generation. She sensed that God was not bound by tradition but was always turning upside down the systems that people devised in God's name.

In J's story, it is the sister-wife and not the brother-husband who had a sense of God's plan. When Rebekah had first realized that she was pregnant with twins, God had warned her that two nations were struggling within her, "and two people born of you shall be divided."[9] To illustrate the wisdom and prophetic insight of a woman, J was using the popular thinking that leadership had passed from the descendants of Esau, the Edomites, to the descendants of Jacob, the Israelites, because the Israelites were more clever and provident. J's first readers would not question God's preference for them over the Edomites. Therefore, they could not question either Rebekah's understanding of God's will or her devious behavior in seeing to it that God's will was done.

Jesus of Nazareth would have recognized Rebekah as one whom he could proudly claim as his sister because she was willing to do the will of God. Like Jesus, Rebekah understood God to have no particular interest in a stable order that would guarantee status according to established rules. If the early Christians looked to the story of Rebekah as an example of what it meant to be a sister in the new family, they would have seen that the community would do well to listen for the prophetic voices of women and to be prepared for constant challenges to established order.

Miriam, Moses, and Aaron

Although many stories about ancient times tell of women with prophetic insight, the first woman in the Bible actually to be called a prophet is Miriam, the older sister of Moses and Aaron.

The first time we see Miriam is in the second chapter of the book we call Exodus, which describes the genocidal effort of Rameses II, the "Pharaoh of the Oppression." Genesis ended with the story of the last of the patriarchs, Isaac's son Joseph, who went from being a spoiled, arrogant teenager to the second-in-command under an Egyptian pharaoh and saved the Egyptians and his own people, whom he brought to Egypt, from starvation in a great famine.

The Book of Exodus begins about three hundred years later with the ominous words, "Now a new king arose over Egypt, who did not know Joseph."[10] By this time the prolific race of Hebrew-speaking foreigners threatened the native people, and the Pharaoh sought to destroy them. After oppressive slavery failed to diminish their numbers, he ordered that every male child should be killed at birth. The mother of Moses, however, was not willing to lose her child. She hid her baby for three months and then devised a plan for his protection and survival. The mother made a papyrus basket, waterproofed it the best she could, put the infant Moses in the basket, and hid it among the reeds on the bank of the river. The mother left her baby, yet she did not entirely abandon him: "His sister stood at a distance, to see what would happen to him."[11]

Miriam was watching. You can imagine the tremulous thoughts that would have passed through the mind of that little slave girl as she waited, knowing that so much rested on her shoulders. She would have been told the story of her people from the time of her weaning. Her mother, Jochebed, had proved herself to be resourceful and passionate for the survival of her people by the means she devised to preserve the life of her infant son. Such a woman would not simply have waited for a son to transmit her passion.[12] Both Miriam and Jochebed knew that the fate of a people was hanging on them. As Miriam looked out fearfully from those bulrushes, she knew she had to find the means of saving her helpless little brother. Perhaps at this moment she had a sense of her significance in history.

Then the daughter of the Pharaoh arrived to bathe. When she spied the little cradle, she sent one of her attendants to fetch it. On opening it, she discovered the baby, who promptly cried and touched her heart. "This must be one of the Hebrews' children," she exclaimed. On cue, Miriam bounced out and announced she knew one of the Hebrew women who would nurse the child for the princess. The princess accepted the offer, and Miriam called her mother. At this point, Miriam fades from the story.

Of course she did not fade from Moses's life. For a while Jochebed had both her children at home. Or maybe she had three of them? The story is not clear about when their brother Aaron was born, but it does say that when Moses was little, Jochebed had her children at home. She could sing to them the songs of their people, tell them the stories of Abraham and Joseph, mark them as Hebrews. Miriam could play with her little brother, hold his hands as he took his first steps, and whisper to him, "I watched over you."

Then Moses was whisked away to the palace of the Pharaoh. Did Miriam ever creep to the palace to glimpse him in ceremonial state? Did she feel a tumult of emotions, a surging of pride, when her brother killed an Egyptian who was battering a Hebrew? Did she feel a deep sense of loss when he fled to Midian?

When Moses returned from Midian, both Aaron and Miriam joined him in leading their people out of their bondage in Egypt. Some people tend to give Moses all the credit for leading the people of Israel to freedom, but when the prophet Micah held up before the people the reminder of what they were called to be—compared to the sorry spectacle of what they had become—he recalled the story in a different way:

> O my people, what have I done to you? In what have I wearied you? Answer me! For I brought you up from the land of Egypt, and redeemed you from the house of slavery; and I sent before you Moses, Aaron, and Miriam.[13]

Over five hundred years after the time of deliverance from slavery, this prophet remembered a woman, the sister, as an equal to Moses and to their brother Aaron. Micah remembered Miriam as a leading participant in God's mighty act of deliverance. The memory of Aaron would have been kept by the powerful house of Levi, the priestly tribe that claimed Moses as a member—but who would have kept the memory of Miriam's name?

The account of the celebration following the successful escape from Egypt suggests an answer to the question of who would have remembered Miriam:

> Then the prophet Miriam, Aaron's sister, took a tambourine in her hand; and all the women went out after her with tambourines and with dancing. And Miriam sang to them: "Sing to the Lord, for he has triumphed gloriously; horse and rider he has thrown into the sea."[14]

On this occasion all the women followed Miriam, and they would have told the story to their daughters and their granddaughters. The phrase "went out after her" helps explain why the women may have remembered Miriam and why some of the men chose to forget her. When women came out in great numbers to sing and dance, they could be a threat to the existing authority. In later years, when the victorious troops of Israel under David's command were returning from a rout of the Philistines, the women also made their presence and their views known:

> The women came out of all the towns of Israel, singing and dancing, to meet King Saul, with tambourines, with songs of joy, and with musical instruments. And the women sang to one another as they made merry, "Saul has killed his thousands, and David his ten thousands." Saul was very angry....[15]

Is it possible that in a later age some men regarded Miriam's hold on the loyalties of the women as a threat to Moses's authority? Is it possible that members of the priestly class, who rewrote the exodus stories long after Micah's affirmation of Miriam's leadership, saw in the memory of Miriam a threat to their own authority?

In the stories as we have received them, the little girl who watched by the river had no public voice, but in the conferences Moses held at night after the failures of the day to persuade Pharaoh to let the people go, Miriam must have been there encouraging, cheering, even analyzing the strategies. Miriam's spontaneous song of victory after the crossing of the sea to freedom sounds as if it came from one who had a part in designing the strategies that prevailed. Her designation as *prophet* attests to a relationship to God that the community affirmed: Moses and Miriam, both prophets.

The last mention of Miriam in the exodus accounts, however, is the strange story of God's repudiation. The story of Miriam's fall from grace appears in the twelfth chapter of Numbers, which contains an account of Miriam's rebellion against the authority of Moses. By this point in the narrative the people have journeyed quite a distance into the inhospitable desert. All the excitement of the successful escape from the Egyptians has faded, and the practical necessities of surviving in this harsh, dry environment have asserted themselves. They begin to long for the easier life of Egypt and to assail Moses with complaints, until in desperation he asks God for some assistance. God replies with a ceremony of investiture in which some of the spirit given to Moses is given to seventy men.

In the very next chapter, we learn of Miriam's mutiny. "What's going on here?" she asks. "How come I've been left out?" Of course that is not the way the Bible puts it. The Bible eases up to the confrontation gradually.

Miriam and Aaron "speak against" Moses because of his Cushite wife. Although Miriam and Aaron could easily have had some negative feelings about their brother's choice of a new wife, such a concern would hardly have been the basis for a rebellion against the authority of Moses. The next verse suggests a more likely reason for Aaron and Miriam's protest:

> They said, "Has the Lord spoken only through Moses?
> Has he not spoken through us also?"[16]

The rest of the story deals with that charge. The Lord hears it and summons all three of them to meet with him outside the camp. Miriam's claim that God has spoken through her is well founded, for she has been called a prophet, so in the story the burden of the Lord's remarks center on the superiority of Moses's calling to hers. After the Lord defends the authority of Moses, the anger of the Lord is kindled against Miriam and Aaron, but only Miriam is punished. When the Lord departs, Miriam becomes white as snow with an affliction called "leprosy."

Aaron pleads with Moses not to lay this sin upon them, but confessing that they have sinned. Moses pleads with God to heal Miriam, and God replies that if her father had cursed her, she would have remained for seven days in confinement, and less cannot be demanded now. So Miriam is shut out of the camp for seven days, and Moses halts the journey until she is brought in again.

What really happened? Miriam may have fallen victim to one of several skin diseases common in that part of the world, but to concentrate our attention on her illness may cause us to miss the real significance of the story. We can only surmise, but as Janice Nunnally-Cox says in her book *Foremothers*, "The narrator, rather than the Lord, seems to have a particular bias against Miriam." Although Miriam and Aaron stand accused of the same offense, only Miriam deserves punishment, apparently because an assertive woman is more offensive than an assertive man. The narrator, fearing the example that such a strong woman might have set for other women, effectively ended her career.

When we contrast the respect for Miriam found in the pronouncements of the eighth-century prophet Micah with the attitude betrayed by the later Priestly writers, we have a good example of how a community can lose sight of a sister's contribution to their history. Even as the story stands, however, the relationship of Miriam to her brothers could have helped early Christians form their understanding of how they were to treat each other in their new family.

Miriam's story begins with her watching over her baby brother. Under normal circumstances of family life, but especially in times of crisis, the older children look after the younger ones. They often have more responsibility than they want to provide for both the protection and training of their little sisters and brothers. In a community that sees itself as a family of equals, without anyone being assigned the role of parent, some will naturally be older and more experienced in life than others. Those with more experience, designated "elders" in early Christian communities, have a special responsibility to pass along their wisdom to both the newer and the younger members of the family.

Miriam organized and led the first celebration following the escape to freedom from slavery in Egypt. In many families, women tend to preside over festival gatherings. As we shall see, Christians in the time of St. Paul followed such customs, with sisters often having the responsibility to organize gatherings of the new family.

The people called Miriam a prophet. They saw that she had a special gift for sensing what God wanted. She had a vision of freedom for her people. Her spiritual descendants among the first Christians were women with a similar gift; their brothers and sisters called them prophets, too. When they prayed or prophesied, these women helped the others to come into God's presence where the family could discover the will of God.

According to the prophet Micah, Miriam shared leadership with her two brothers. That arrangement may have been in St. Paul's mind when he addressed a letter to the three leaders of a church: Philemon, Apphia, and Archippus. By calling it simply the Letter to Philemon, later Christians may have failed to see that their predecessors in the faith found strength in brothers and sisters sharing leadership responsibility just as did the people of Israel in their quest for freedom.

Miriam and her brothers quarreled. When the boys were small, Miriam as the older sister would have exercised authority in the family that was limited only by their mother's interventions. Then the little brothers grew up and took charge. The older of the two resented the continued assertiveness of his sister, and she objected to his authoritarian ways. Miriam, Moses, and Aaron in their quarrels sound much like any other family of gifted children who grow up to be leaders. Surely, the early followers of Jesus were aware of the potential rivalries and jealousies they were creating by seeing themselves as sis-

ters and brothers. The new family would incorporate
many of the problems people thought they were leaving
behind when they shifted their loyalties away from the
families into which they had been born. Sadly enough,
from the perspective of the late twentieth century, the
Christians in the second century took the path chosen by
the Priestly writers who rewrote Miriam's story. They
sought to eliminate the rivalry by denying women the
right to positions of authority and leadership.

Intimacy without Arousal

Brothers and sisters naturally struggle with one another.
Theirs is a relationship of equals. In a healthy family the
natural conflict between sisters and brothers ultimately
produces trust, caring, vulnerability, and honesty. In ancient times the religious leaders of the Jewish people
thought it was important to protect that relationship by
codifying the rules that most people had arrived at
through instinct and experience. The rules governing the
behavior of brothers and sisters toward each other appear
in Leviticus:

> None of you shall approach anyone near of kin to un-
> cover nakedness: I am the Lord....You shall not uncover
> the nakedness of your sister, your father's daughter or
> your mother's daughter, whether born at home or born
> abroad....You shall not uncover the nakedness of your fa-
> ther's wife's daughter, begotten by your father, since
> she is your sister. If a man takes his sister, a daughter of
> his father or a daughter of his mother, and sees her na-
> kedness, and she sees his nakedness, it is a disgrace, and
> they shall be cut off in the sight of their people; he has
> uncovered his sister's nakedness, he shall be subject to
> punishment.[17]

Rules against sexual activity between brothers and sisters are nearly universal. They can be explained as conditioned behavior that assures a healthy gene pool and
prevents the recurrence of undesirable traits arising from
inbreeding. The instinctive nature of the sexual distance

that exists in a healthy intimacy between sisters and brothers is evident in the co-educational dormitories on college campuses. Many women will not date the men who live in rooms next to theirs or even on their floor. They say that they think of the men living close to them as brothers and rarely have sexual fantasies about them. Some men report much the same experience in regard to the women, who become like sisters to them. This biologically conditioned behavior toward people of the opposite sex living in close quarters apparently created problems for the couples in China who were wed as small children and reared together in the same household. Many of these couples experienced difficulty in producing offspring. Having been raised as brothers and sisters, they did not arouse each other's sexual appetites.

If brothers and sisters have a biologically inherited aversion to sexual contact with each other, we might wonder why the people of Israel needed a law prohibiting them from doing the unthinkable. With a little reflection, however, we can find two reasons for putting such a law on the books.

In the first place, the antipathy toward sexual activity between brothers and sisters appears to be generated by living in proximity to one another rather than on actual genetic kinship. That is why the sexual code in Leviticus emphasizes that rules against incest between brothers and sisters apply "whether born at home or born abroad." Sisters and brothers who do not meet until they are adults do not have the natural protection against inbreeding that they would have received had they been reared together. The law also covers relationships between half-brothers and half-sisters. When polygamy was the common practice, children of the same father but different mothers often grew up in separate households. As a consequence of their separation through early childhood, they would not have had an opportunity to develop defenses against the possibility of sexual attraction to one another. As we will see, the only case of sibling incest reported in Hebrew

Scriptures occurred between a young man and his half-sister.

The second reason for the law arose because human beings can override their instincts and indulge in socially destructive behavior. The people of ancient Israel may well have faced enough problems with incest for them to codify what they thought was a reasonable standard of behavior. They wrote laws to keep people in line with what was best for the tribe or the community. They were convinced that the love between sisters and brothers must be based on intimacy without the complications of sexual arousal.

When Jesus called his followers sisters and brothers, from their familiarity with Jewish law they knew exactly what he meant. They were to form intimate connections with one another but to curb their sexual appetites. Doing the will of the Father would include treating each other as if they had grown up in the same household. They were not to manipulate each other by seductiveness or to abuse each other by sexual aggressiveness. They were to base their behavior toward each other on the kind of trust, caring, vulnerability, and honesty that characterize the best of relationships between brothers and sisters.

The Sister-Wives

The complicated nature of the relationship between sisters and their brothers seems to lie behind three strange stories in Genesis about patriarchs who said that their wives were their sisters.

In the first of these stories, Abraham took his family to Egypt during a famine in his own land. When they arrived in Egypt, he said to his wife Sarah, "I know well that you are a woman beautiful in appearance; and when the Egyptians see you, they will say, 'This is his wife'; then they will kill me, but they will let you live. Say you are my sister, so that it may go well with me because of you, and that my life may be spared on your account."[18] The ruse worked all too well. Pharaoh learned of Sarah's beauty and took her into his harem. Soon, however, the Lord afflicted

54

the Egyptians with great plagues, and when Pharaoh discovered the reason, he sent Abraham and Sarah away.

In a similar encounter, this time with the king of Gerar, Abraham claimed that calling his wife his sister was not just a ruse but a fact. He told King Abimelech that Sarah was his sister, so the king took Sarah into his household. Before Abimelech "approached her," however, God warned him in a dream that she was married and the next morning Abimelech confronted Abraham:

> "What have you done to us? How have I sinned against you, that you have brought such great guilt on me and my kingdom? You have done things to me that ought not to be done." And Abimelech said to Abraham, "What were you thinking of, that you did this thing?" Abraham said, "I did it because I thought, There is no fear of God at all in this place, and they will kill me because of my wife. Besides, *she is indeed my sister*, the daughter of my father but not the daughter of my mother; and she became my wife."[19]

In the third story about men who identify their wives as sisters, it is not Abraham but his son Isaac who lived for a time in Gerar and tried to protect himself by claiming that his beautiful wife was his sister. In this version of the story, no dream was required to let King Abimelech know that he was being deceived by a foreigner. The king "looked out of a window and saw him fondling his wife Rebekah."[20] In both the Abraham and Isaac stories located in Gerar, Abimelech, after an angry accusation, allowed the patriarch and his household to remain in his land.

Apparently neither the editors of Genesis nor their sources fully appreciated the Egyptian origins of the stories. In Egypt an exception was made to the general prohibition of sexual relations between siblings. The members of Egyptian royal families could forge marriages between brothers and sisters. In their ability to transcend their biologically-conditioned sexual aversion for each other, royal brothers and sisters demonstrated their superiority to the common people. Probably in the earliest form of the ancient folk tales, the patriarchs and matriarchs of the Jewish people were shown to be the equals of Egyptian royalty.

Although the editors of Genesis may not have understood the original point of the sister-wife folk tales, they must have found them especially intriguing since they used the same plot three times. They may have been fascinated by the idea that the legendary ancestors of the Jews had trouble transcending the sexual limitations generally imposed on brothers and sisters married to each other. According to Genesis, both Sarah and Rebekah were barren. Neither was able to get pregnant without divine intervention.[21] The stories about the sister-wives may have been a way of reminding people of what they already knew to be true: sisters and brothers do not have a natural sexual attraction to each other.

The reminder that a normal relationship between a sister and her brother excludes sexual arousal may have been useful to the early Christians, but other aspects of the sister-wife stories may have added more to their understanding of what Jesus meant by calling a woman his sister.

In each of the stories, the men appear to be something less than exemplary characters. They understood that the prohibition against adultery in the foreign lands in which they were living offered them no protection. If the monarch wanted a married woman, he would simply kill the husband before taking the woman into his harem. To save their own lives they were willing not only to lie about the nature of their relationship to their sisters, they were also willing to let the women endure the moral degradation of an adulterous liaison with a lecherous king.

In contrast to the men, the women show great courage and strength of character. They will do whatever is necessary to protect their defenseless brother-husbands—endure the isolation of harem life, accept the shame of adultery, and even risk the wrath of God. These women blazed the trail that centuries later Jesus of Nazareth would follow in doing what he perceived to be the will of the Father. For the sake of the anxious and helpless people he loved, he would endure utter loneliness, the agony of separation from God, and the shame of the cross.

The sister-wives play something more than minor parts in stories featuring the patriarchs. As we have seen, Rebekah proved herself to be wiser than Isaac in providing for the future of the clan. Previously, her mother-in-law Sarah had also taken strong measures to assure that leadership would pass to the appropriate son, eliminating the possibility that the chosen son might be challenged by his half-brother.[22] Although they have to work around the strictures imposed by a patriarchal society, these women exercised the authority of full partners in their marriages. They were not the subservient, dependent type of wives sometimes idealized by subsequent generations.

The sister-wife does not appear again in the pages of the Bible until we come to St. Paul's first letter to the Christian community in Corinth. In this passage Paul is claiming for himself and his companions the same rights granted "the other apostles and the brothers of the Lord and Cephas."[23] One of those prerogatives was to be accompanied by an *adelphe gune*, literally, a "sister-wife" or a "sister-woman." When we examine Paul's attitude toward the women of the church, we will see that his understanding of the wife as sister is remarkably similar to what we have found in Genesis. Although in this same letter Paul opposes sexual abstinence for married couples, he understood that women were to be full partners with their husbands in marriage, and that partnership included travel in the service of the Lord. The married women who were friends of Paul, such as Priscilla, were independent people of the Sarah and Rebekah type.

Dinah and Her Brothers

Sisters and brothers also have a natural desire to protect one another. The protective nature of the sister and brother relationship is reflected in the legends that found their way into the Hebrew Scriptures. The story of Miriam illustrates the protective instincts of a big sister toward her baby brother. Later in the story Moses looked after

Miriam: he made the whole company of Israel pause in their journey while Miriam completed her confinement outside of the camp. In much the same fashion, the story of Dinah demonstrates the violently protective potential of brothers when their sister is mistreated.

Dinah, the daughter of Leah and Jacob, went out to visit the women of the region where the clan was camped at the time. When Shechem, son of Hamor the Hivite, prince of the region, saw her, "his soul was drawn to Dinah," but rather than court her he abducted and raped her. When Dinah's brothers heard about their sister's defilement by the son of the local warlord, they were furious. Before they had time to react, Shechem approached them with an offer:

> "Let me find favor with you, and whatever you say to me
> I will give. Put the marriage present and gift as high as
> you like, and I will give whatever you ask me; only give
> me the girl to be my wife."[24]

Apparently Shechem had fallen in love with the young women he had so viciously raped. Jacob did not want to make trouble and would probably have accepted Shechem's proposal, but Dinah's two full brothers, Simeon and Levi, took matters into their own hands. In negotiating with Shechem and his father Hamor, the brothers insisted that to give their sister to an uncircumcised man would be a disgrace for them. They demanded that not only Shechem but all the men of their city be circumcised. Because Shechem was "the most honored of all his family," Hamor agreed to the conditions for the marriage. Then on the third day after their painful operations, when the men were still incapacitated, Simeon and Levi launched a surprise attack on the city. They killed all the men, including Hamor and his son Shechem, and rescued their sister Dinah.

Her father was not pleased even though the attack and rescue mission had been completely successful. He pointed out to Simeon and Levi that their clan, being small in number, could not afford to make enemies of the people who were inhabitants of the land in which they were temporarily residing. If the Canaanites and the Perizzites formed an alliance against them, they could easily be destroyed. His sons were unrepentant, however, and responded with the question, "Should our sister be treated like a whore?"

Many male readers of the story up through the first half of the twentieth century would probably have felt that Shechem was trying to do the "right thing" by offering to marry the woman he had raped, especially since he was in love with her. That method of dealing with the problem was even enshrined in the laws of Deuteronomy: "If a man meets a virgin who is not engaged, and seizes her and lies with her, and they are caught in the act, the man who lay with her shall give fifty shekels of silver to the young woman's father, and she shall become his wife. Because he violated her he shall not be permitted to divorce her as long as he lives."[25] It sounds outrageous to modern ears that a woman could be forced to spend the rest of her life with a man who had violated her, but that was the law and the custom for centuries.

What is noteworthy about the story of Dinah and her brothers Simeon and Levi is that the young men refused to follow these accepted customs in responding to rape. Instead they risked their lives, put the safety of their clan in jeopardy, and incurred the wrath of their father in order to rescue their sister. Obviously those who told this story did not think highly of the opinion that somehow marriage would undo the wrong committed by rape. People who opposed such oppressive practices might not have been able to rewrite the laws or change the customs, but they could tell powerful stories to remind their readers that sexual violence is beyond the pale and deserving of severe, even violent, punishment. In the stories of the Bible, loving brothers do not permit their sisters to become perpetual victims of the men who rape them.

Tamar, Amnon, and Absalom

Further on in the Hebrew Scriptures, another brother with similar loyalty to his sister appears on the scene—Absalom and his sister Tamar. In this account, however, the perpetrator of a violent act against Tamar is also her brother, Amnon. Actually, he is a half-brother, probably reared in a separate household from that of his half-sister. All three were children of King David, but the brother who committed the vicious crime had a different mother from the other two.

King David's large family was not remembered as being an especially happy one. When Jesus chose family imagery to describe relationships in a new community, he was aware that he could not hold up all the families described in the Hebrew Scriptures as models for what he had in mind. In fact, his denunciation of natural families provides evidence enough that he understood how families pass on destructive patterns of behavior from generation to generation. The story of David and his children illustrates how a family perpetuates misery when a son picks up the worst of the father's traits.

2 Samuel 11 and 12 narrate the story of David's sin against one of his soldiers, Uriah. There was a battle going on, but David, we are told, remained in Jerusalem. One day after a nap David was walking on the roof of his house and spied Bathsheba performing her monthly ablutions. She was very beautiful, and David's passion ran high. He sent one of his people to find out who she was and had her brought to him. They slept together, and shortly thereafter she sent word to David that she was pregnant.

Upon hearing this, David concocted a cunning scheme. He invited her husband Uriah to the palace and sent him to his house with presents. Uriah, however, faithful son of Israel, did not go down to his house but slept at the entrance to the palace with the servants. When David was informed of this, he demanded of Uriah why he had not taken advantage of the respite granted him and spent the night with his wife. Uriah, innocent that he was, replied that the precious religious symbols of their people and the faithful soldiers were camping in the open field; at such a time, he could not enjoy sexual pleasures with his wife. David tried again the next night, plying him with food and drink until he became drunk, but still Uriah did not go down to his wife. Desperate, David sent by Uriah's hand a letter to his general telling him to place Uriah in a position of certain death.

When Bathsheba heard of her husband's death, she made the proper ritual observance of mourning, and she and David were married and had their son. Then the wrath of God in the form of his wild prophet Nathan descended on David. The prophet denounced David's sin and promised that the child of this union would die and that furthermore the sword would never depart from David's house. It is in this troubled house that the story of Tamar, Absalom, and their half-brother Amnon unfolds.

Amnon falls in love with his beautiful half-sister Tamar. He becomes so obsessed with her that he makes himself physically ill, assuming that because of their kinship she is beyond his reach. Amnon's crafty cousin, Jonadab, notices that he is looking haggard and inquires as to the reason. When Amnon confesses that he is in love with Tamar, Jonadab suggests a plan for getting Tamar into bed:

> "Lie down on your bed, and pretend to be ill; and when your father comes to see you, say to him, 'Let my sister Tamar come and give me something to eat, and prepare the food in my sight, so that I may see it and eat it from her hand.'"[26]

Amnon follows his cousin's advice to the letter. When his father David pays a visit to his ailing son, Amnon asks him to let Tamar come and bring him food. So Tamar goes to Amnon's house where she prepares cakes from the dough she had brought with her while he watches her from his bed. When the cakes are ready, she brings them over to his bed, but he refuses to eat. Instead he orders everyone out of the house, and then insists that Tamar feed him. The innocent Tamar, with the food in her hands, comes up to the bed. Absalom grabs her and tries to pull her down onto the bed insisting, "Come, lie with me, my sister."

Tamar resists. She not only reminds Amnon that such a thing is not done in Israel, but also that there is a legitimate outlet for his desire. They are a royal family; the laws against incest do not apply. "Speak to the King," she says, "for he would not withhold me from you." She reminds him that not only she would suffer, but he would be "one of the fools in Israel," as the King James Version puts it. But no words can deter this violent man. "He would not listen to her, and being stronger than she, he forced her and lay with her." Phyllis Trible, in *Texts of Terror*, says the Hebrew is even stronger, more suggestive of contempt: "He laid her."

The rape scene is over quickly. What follows is even more horrible. Amnon is seized with a great loathing for her. Indeed, says the text, the hate with which he hated her was even greater than the love with which he had loved her. "Get out," he tells Tamar. He no longer calls her "sister."

The strength of Tamar is remarkable. She remains clear about the situation, calm and reasonable—wisdom incarnate. "No, my brother," she responds, "this wrong in sending me away is greater than the other that you did to me." Again he would not listen, but summoned an attendant. Most translations read, "Put this woman out of my presence," but Trible says that the Hebrew has only the demonstrative pronoun: "Put this out of my sight." Tamar has become a thing to him. Tamar stumbles away, tearing her virgin's robe and crying, the ashes of humiliation on her head. By her actions she makes public her disgrace. She will not participate in any attempt to cover up the crime.

Her full brother Absalom now appears in the story. He understands at once what has happened. "Be quiet for now, my sister," he counsels. "Do not take this to heart." His advice on the surface seems heartless, but notice the words *for now*. The time for justice will come.

In contrast to David and Amnon, Absalom is Tamar's vindicator. He takes his abused sister into his house, and there she remains in sanctuary for two years. The king's only response is that he becomes "very angry." With whom? For what? He will not punish Amnon because he is his firstborn and he loves him. Absalom begins to plot his revenge. "He speaks to Amnon neither good nor bad for two years," the narrator tells us, "for Absalom hated Amnon, because he had raped his sister Tamar."

Then after two full years his opportunity comes. Justice against Amnon does not need to be swift, but it must be sure. It is the time of the festival of the sheepshearing. Absalom prepares a feast and invites all the king's sons. David has reservations about Amnon's going, but Absalom persuades him. At the height of the festivities, at Absalom's command, his men kill Amnon, and panic ensues. The other sons, fearful of this handsome, brooding, ambitious prince, mount their mules and flee. Word comes to David that all his sons have been killed, and the ritual acts of desolation follow. The shrewd counselor, who accurately took David's measure in making possible the rape, then explains to David what has happened. "Let not my lord suppose that they have killed all the young men the king's sons; Amnon alone is dead. This has been determined by Absalom from the day Amnon raped his sister Tamar."[27]

This is a graphic and terrible story. Nowhere is the threat uttered by the prophet Nathan more perfectly realized: "The sword shall never depart from your house."[28] The death of Amnon, however, does not mark an end to killing within the family of King David. Later Absalom would organize a rebellion against his father's rule and would himself die by the sword in an attempt to make himself king.

David was a gifted soldier, politician, and administrator. He unified and made a nation of the twelve competing tribes of Israel, but he failed miserably as a father. As is the case with all too many successful and powerful men, David decided that the rules did not apply to him; he was above the law. He would stop at nothing, not even the murder of a loyal subject, to get the woman he wanted for his bed. David's sons showed few signs that they might have inherited his talent for leadership. Even the widely acclaimed wisdom of Solomon was not sufficient to keep the nation from disintegration. The sons followed in David's footsteps most obviously when they tried to take what they wanted without concern for law, custom, or the rights of other people, even members of their own family.

The most admirable of David's children may well have been his daughter Tamar. Phyllis Trible, in her commentary on the story of Amnon's assault of his sister, brilliantly analyzes the account not only for its language but also for the power of its structure. She calls the story "The Royal Rape of Wisdom," for Tamar speaks the only words of wisdom in the scene. She reminds Amnon that what he intends is a thing not done in Israel. She even shows him that if his affection for her is genuine, he has a legitimate alternative to pursue. After Amnon orders her away, the judgment she pronounces has the ring of a prophet's truth. Then, instead of creeping away and hiding her shame, the innocent victim of a brutal assault makes a public display of her grief.

Christian writers have made much of David as the spiritual, if not the actual, ancestor of Jesus, but in his words and actions Jesus of Nazareth had little in common with this cruel and grasping king. In the stories about David and his family, the person Jesus most resembles is Tamar. Like Tamar, Jesus spoke the truth that others did not want to hear; like her, he was an innocent person who was despised and rejected and who became a public spectacle as his life was destroyed.

Tamar's brother Absalom, although as ambitious and brutal as their father David, would not stand aside and passively observe his sister's pain. He saw to it that justice was done, and he was gentle with his sister. He took her into his house and made her one of his family. The author of 2 Samuel speaks this way of Absalom's loyalty to his sister: "There were born to Absalom three sons, and one daughter whose name was Tamar; she was a beautiful woman."[29] The brother would keep green and undefiled the memory of his sister.

Absalom's story helped subsequent generations understand what it means to be a brother, and along with the brothers of Dinah, he set a standard for those who call themselves "brothers" in Christian communities. Brothers do not tolerate unwelcome sexual attention paid to their sisters; they do not look the other way when their sisters are assaulted; they will do whatever is necessary to rescue their sisters from sexual abuse and bring the perpetrator to justice. Unfortunately, many men who think of themselves as Christians have refused to think of sexually mistreated women as their sisters. Forcing women into marriage with their abusers, they have followed the standards of Leviticus and ignored the deeper wisdom of the brother-sister stories. In trying to protect each other from punishment, they have tried to make women responsible for the sexual assaults they have suffered, too often doing far too little to provide comfort and protection.

These ancient Hebrew stories about sisters and brothers appeared in the only sacred writings acknowledged by the first Christian communities. Their understanding of themselves as a family was conditioned by the brother and sister stories they believed had been preserved to show them the way. "These things happened to them to serve as an example, and they were written down to instruct us," asserted Paul in writing to the church in Corinth.[30] The word translated here as "example" is *tupos* in the Greek used by Paul. The root of our word "type," it originally meant a blow, as from an ax, but later came to mean the mark left by the blow. For Paul and the other Christians of his generation, the Hebrew Scriptures provided marks along the way, like trail blazes in the woods, to keep them from getting lost as they tried to fulfill the radical vision of community that Jesus held: a new family of sisters and brothers living as equals.

In the new family, women's insight would be as respected as that of men. Knowing the story of Rebekah's wisdom in choosing a leader for the next generation, the community could assume that the will of God for them could as easily be revealed through a woman as a man. Miriam would be a reminder that women could be prophets and leaders. In marriage and in church life, married women were not to be seen merely as wives, but also to be "sisters," like Sarah and Rebekah, full partners both in their households and in the community.

If they saw themselves as sisters and brothers, women and men in the church would be able to find standards of behavior that would allow them to work closely with one another and to look after one another. They would offer each other not only guidance, but nurture and protection. Keeping in mind a concern for future generations, they would follow the example of Laban and Rebekah, and help each other with the rearing of children.

Some of the "marks" Christians could find in the Hebrew Scriptures pointed the way along the path they were to follow while others served as warning signs. If they did not pay attention, the new family they were forming could take on all of the destructive characteristics of natural families. Rebekah's use of devious means to assert her authority stands as a reminder of what women are forced to do when men deny them full partnership in the church. Miriam and Aaron's rebellion against Moses can be seen as a similar danger sign for those who do not want to share authority with their brothers and sisters in the community. The story of David's family points out how destructive patterns of behavior can be passed along from generation to generation, not only in natural families but in the church.

Both the positive and negative examples of family life that appear in the Hebrew Scriptures helped the first Christians develop an understanding of what Jesus meant when he told his followers that they were to be sisters and brothers. The letters of St. Paul will illustrate how they put that metaphor to good use.

Endnotes

1. Harold Bloom and David Rosenberg, *The Book of J* (New York: Vintage Books, 1991), p. 35.

2. *Ibid.*, p. 32.

3. Gen. 24:55.

4. Gen. 25:27-28.

5. Gen. 27:1-29

6. Gen. 27:43-45.

7. Gen. 29:13-14.

8. Gen. 26:1-11.

9. Gen. 25:23.

10. Exod. 1:8.

11. Exod. 2:4.

12. Jochebed is named in Exod. 6:20 and Num. 26:59.

13. Mic. 6:3-4.

14. Exod. 15:20-21.

15. 1 Sam. 18:6-8.

16. Num. 12:2.

17. Lev. 18:6,9,11; 20:17.

18. Gen. 12:11-13.

19. Gen. 20:9-12.

20. Gen. 26:8.

21. Gen. 18:9-15 and 25:21.

22. Gen. 21:8-14

23. 1 Cor. 9:5.

24. Gen. 34:11-12.

25. Deut. 22:28-29.

26. 2 Sam. 13:5.

27. 2 Sam. 13:32.

28. 2 Sam. 12:10.

29. 2 Sam. 14:27.

30. 1 Cor. 10:11.

Chapter 3

St. Paul's Family of Equals

When St. Paul and his companions brought the news of Jesus and his teaching to Gentiles, they declared that the Lord they worshiped wanted all people to be equal. St. Paul held that everyone—male and female, Jew and Gentile, slave and free—could become God's adopted children, but not every follower of Jesus agreed with him. Some of the Christians in Jerusalem insisted that Gentiles were not fit to become followers of Jesus unless they were willing to become Jews. In arguing that God made no distinction between Gentiles and Jews, Paul expanded his theory of equality to include two other groups that conventional thinking held to be inferior, slaves and women. In his letter to the Christians in Galatia he wrote, "There is no longer Jew or Greek, there is no longer slave or free, there is no longer male and female; for all of you are one in Christ Jesus."[1]

Although in his letter to the Galatians Paul was concentrating his attention on the relationship between Jews and Gentiles in the church, his line of argument revealed his convictions about the relationship between women and men. If Greeks could be adopted children of God just as they were, without being second-class citizens, so could women. In pursuing his line of reasoning that all people equally stand in need of redemption, Paul went out of his way to remind his readers that without the contribution of a particular woman, they would not be a community at all.

God had sent his son, "born of a woman," to set them free for adoption as God's rightful heirs.[2]

To proclaim this equality between male and female, Paul and the other early Christians latched on to a metaphor that they derived from the teachings of Jesus himself. They called each other "sister" or "brother," *adelphe* or *adelphos*, literally, those "from the same womb."

New translations of the Bible have made an important contribution to our understanding of these New Testament terms. In the New Revised Standard Version, for example, when *adelphos* is used in a general sense, it is often translated "brother or sister," and *adelphoi* frequently becomes "brothers and sisters" instead of the familiar "brethren" found in the King James Version or "brothers" used in later English translations.

At some points in the text, instead of adding "sisters" to the "brothers," modern translators have employed gender-neutral words or phrases. *Adelphos* has now become "neighbor," "member of the church," or "disciple." In the original Greek of the New Testament, when followers of Jesus are called the *adelphoi*, the English equivalents now include students, family, friends, believers, community, beloved, or comrades.[3] In order to make a distinction between Christians and the rest of the Jewish people, the translators have found still other inclusive words for *adelphoi* when the author is writing about the Jews—such as Israelites, relatives, kinsfolk, kindred, and people.

The great variety of English words used to translate "from the same womb" provides us with a better understanding of the connotations and nuances revealed in the metaphor than "brother" or "brethren" do. The contribution to our understanding, however, has obscured the centrality of the metaphor in the lives of the first Christians. St. Paul and the authors of the gospels and of the Acts of the Apostles constantly and consistently use the sister-brother metaphor in writing about the followers of Jesus. When translators substitute other words, they may create a smooth, gender-neutral rendering of a passage, but they also conceal the central symbol of the new community's understanding of how individuals were to treat each other. The language of New Testament reveals the self-understanding of the early church. By referring to themselves as sisters and brothers, these men and women were making a statement about how they intended to organize themselves and to treat each other. In using family imagery, the early Christians might simply have been following a popular custom, for often disciples of a revered teacher called themselves *adelphoi*. But the disciples of Jesus had more than custom shaping their way of thinking about themselves. They remembered the vision of community that Jesus had put before them, and they passed on the vision to new recruits. One of these new recruits, who had never met Jesus in the flesh, seems to have understood the radical implications of that vision even better than the men in the original company of Jesus's followers. His name was Paul.

The Apostle Paul

Like Jesus, Paul grew up in a family with at least one sister. According to the Acts of the Apostles, his sister's son once saved him from being ambushed and killed.[4] The Roman tribune in Jerusalem had arrested Paul for inciting a riot and placed him under detention at the barracks. The tribune, wanting to find out what the local people had against Paul, ordered him to appear before the chief priests and the entire council for questioning. Paul so enraged some of these interrogators that they formed a conspiracy to ambush and kill him as he was being brought back to the council from the barracks on the next day of his examination. Somehow Paul's nephew learned of the plot and gained access to the barracks to warn Paul. Paul talked one of the centurions into taking the young man to the tribune to report what he had heard. On the basis of this intelligence, the tribune arranged for Paul to slip out of Jerusalem at night with a well-armed escort.

If this brief episode has any historical validity, Paul would have known the importance of family loyalty. Having a sister, he would also have understood the limitations of conventional family life that caused Jesus to urge his followers to leave their natural families and to become sisters and brothers in a new family.

Many people who possess only a superficial knowledge of the Bible are surprised to hear that Paul advocated equality between men and women. They have heard, after all, that Paul was a notorious misogynist. Did he not say that women are to keep silent in church? Did he not require women to be subject to their husbands? Was it not Paul who refused permission for a woman to teach or have authority over a man? Before we can examine his letters and the Acts of the Apostles for evidence of Paul's understanding of the new community advocated by Jesus, we will have to look more closely at these popular misconceptions of Paul's teaching.

In the first place, not all of these letters were written by Paul. Some of the letters in the New Testament attributed to Paul were in all probability actually written a generation or two after his death. In vocabulary, style, and content the letters to Timothy and Titus do not sound at all like the Paul we have come to know through his letters to the Romans, Corinthians, Galatians, Philippians, and Thessalonians. Whether Paul or one of his followers wrote the letters to the Ephesians or the Colossians is a matter of debate. Without question, the letters to Timothy and Titus, and to a lesser extent the letters to the Colossians and to the Ephesians, consign women to a traditional subservient role, but we do Paul a grave injustice if we assign to him responsibility for missing Jesus's point that his followers were to live as sisters and brothers.

In the second place, people who quote letters generally acknowledged to be from Paul often ignore the context in which they found the objectionable opinion. For example, let us look at the letter that Paul wrote to the Christians in Corinth stating that "women should be silent in the churches."[5] The admonition appears as a parenthetical remark in the midst of Paul's comments on the relative merits of prophesying and "speaking in tongues." Paul held

71

that those who prophesy "speak to other people for their upbuilding and encouragement and consolation," while those who speak in a tongue speak only to God, "for nobody understands them."[6]

What these "tongues" might have been is a matter of some conjecture. One commentator adept in both psychology and biblical criticism has said that "tongues" were probably the incoherent babbling of people who were expressing "a backlog of fear" carried over from the earliest days of childhood before speech was possible.[7] He saw a value in the practice because of the strong link between speaking in tongues and contemplative prayer—both are irrational and both stress God as being beyond knowing. Many forms of contemplative prayer also employ vocalization without regard for the logic of words, such as chanting in a foreign language or repeating a single word or phrase. Paul had no objection to the practice of uttering meaningless sounds as long as things did not get out of hand and dominate the gatherings. So that all things might "be done decently and in order," Paul urged silence in certain situations. If no one could interpret or make sense out of the sounds for the edification of the community, the person who wanted to speak in a tongue was to be silent. Paul much preferred that people speak intelligibly.

In the middle of this discourse on speaking in tongues and prophesying, we find Paul's famous lines that have marked him as a misogynist:

> As in all the churches of the saints, women should be silent in the churches. For they are not permitted to speak, but should be subordinate, as the law also says. If there is anything they desire to know, let them ask their husbands at home. For it is shameful for a woman to speak in church. Or did the word of God originate with you? Or are you the only ones it has reached?[8]

We should note that Paul was not urging all women to keep silence in regard to speaking in tongues, but only those with husbands. English translations have obscured the fact that Paul was writing about married women and not about women in general. The word for "women" could just as well be translated "wives." Greek had only one word for both woman and wife: *gune*. Paul thought that married women should not get mixed up with this business of speaking in tongues, either by doing it or by trying to make sense out of the babbling of another person. Paul might well have been worried that speaking in tongues could create a rift between married people. They might start arguing in public and create a scene.

Although Paul did not want wives to argue with their husbands, he wanted them to prophesy. In fact, he wrote that while the Corinthians were to tolerate speaking in tongues, he wanted them "all" to prophesy.[9] In telling the married women in Corinth to be silent in church, Paul must have been writing about the advisability of silence in regard to the particular business of speaking in tongues, and not about a general rule of silence for wives, because he concluded his argument with these words:

> So, my *brothers and sisters*, be eager to prophesy, and
> do not forbid speaking in tongues; but all things should
> be done decently and in order.[10]

Paul wanted everything done "in order." The word in Greek is *tasso*. He abhorred disorder, *akatastasia*, which he considered to be contrary to God's nature. He wanted everyone in the church to be subject to, or subordinate to, order: *hupotasso*. In the parenthetical comment in question, the words do not say that the wives are to be subordinate to the order of their husbands, but simply that they should be subject to order, presumably the order established by God.

If Paul wrote that married women should be subject to order, why did he single them out for special treatment? What about the widows, the single women, or the men? Everyone is equally capable of causing a disruption in the church, but Paul may have experienced the particular anguish of watching a woman tear her husband to emotional shreds during an argument in public. Paul respected women, and his respect carried with it a bit of fear. He might well have urged married women to save their arguments with their husbands until they could be alone in the privacy of their own houses. If Paul is more concerned here with the public behavior of women than of men, and if he reacts to arguments between wives and husbands from a narrow point of view, that would make his insistence on equality between men and women all the more remarkable.

Women and Men as Prophets

Paul wanted the women as well as the men to prophesy. Earlier in his letter to the Corinthians, before he addressed the subject of speaking in tongues, he had gone on at some length about how both women and men were to arrange their hair when they led public worship. "Any man who prays or prophesies with something on his head disgraces his head, but any woman who prays or prophesies with her head unveiled disgraces her head—it is one and the same thing as having her head shaved."[11] Scholars have been debating for years the exact meaning of these words, but our concern here is not whether Paul was referring to veils or hats or hair styles. The point is that he recognized women as well as men as prophets in the church, and wanted to remind them about the importance of their appearance in public.

While urging the prophets, both men and women, to be conscious of their appearance, Paul made an unequivocal statement about the equality of men and women. After reminding them that man "is the image and reflection of God," he referred to the story of woman being taken from man in Genesis 2:21-22, but he did not want his readers to think that he followed the traditional Jewish argument about the chronological priority of men:

> In the Lord woman is not independent of man or man independent of woman. For just as woman came from man, so man comes through woman; but all things come from God.[12]

By using the phrase "in the Lord," Paul was insisting that
in church men and women are completely equal. Because
of what they had learned from Jesus, Christians now perceived that childbirth was an expression of God's intention that men and women should be equal. As one scholar
writes: "The same God who created woman from the side
of man is also responsible for the fact that man comes
from a woman's womb."[13] Christians were not to make a
distinction between the authority of men and women
prophets.

The Acts of the Apostles also reflects the customs of the
church in Paul's time when women as well as men were
leaders of the spiritual life of the early Christian communities, as in this description of the daughters of Philip:

> The next day we left and came to Caesarea; and we
> went into the house of Philip the evangelist, one of the
> seven, and stayed with him. He had four unmarried
> daughters who had the gift of prophecy.[14]

The daughters of Philip left Caesarea and continued their
ministries in Hierapolis, according to two second-century
sources.[15] The stories about them provide further evidence
that women functioned as prophets in the early church
and spoke to gathered communities. These women carried
on the tradition of the prophet Miriam, who shared the
leadership of Israel with her brothers Moses and Aaron
and who led the people in their celebration of their escape to freedom.

The "Sisters" of St. Paul

Paul's attitude toward women comes through his letters
more clearly when he writes about a particular woman
rather than about women in general. For example, in the
opening lines of his letter to the Corinthians he says:

> Now I appeal to you, brothers and sisters, by the name
> of our Lord Jesus Christ, that all of you be in agreement
> and that there be no divisions among you, but that you
> be united in the same mind and the same purpose. For it

has been reported to me by Chloe's people that there
are quarrels among you, my brothers and sisters.[16]

Chloe's name does not appear again in Paul's letters or in
any of the other ancient records of the church, but by calling attention to her at the beginning of his letter to the
quarrelsome Corinthians, Paul has given us a valuable
glimpse into the workings of the early church. Chloe was
a leader of sufficient stature to have a group of people in
the church identified with her name—"Chloe's people."
They may have met at her house, or she may have been
their mentor, or perhaps Chloe provided both space and
leadership for a gathering of those attracted to the teachings of Jesus. Whatever the reason they were identified
with her name, Chloe's people had a reputation that Paul
assumed would have an impact on the people receiving
his letter.

As Paul continues his complaints about the factions developing in the church at Corinth, he implies that the people who identified with Chloe had a better understanding
of Jesus's message than did those who identified with
Apollos or Cephas or even Paul himself. Paul laments that
some say, "I belong to Paul," or "I belong to Apollos," or "I
belong to Cephas," but he does not accuse Chloe's people
of this kind of factionalism.

Chloe may have been one of many women who were
essential to Paul's missionary strategy, independent
women who had the resources necessary for organizing a
Christian cell. The letter to the Colossians may include a
fragment of a genuine letter from Paul, which is a message
to another such woman, and this time he specifically
states that a group of Christians gathered in her house:
"Give my greetings to the brothers and sisters in Laodicea,
and to Nympha and the church in her house."[17]

Some congregations had more than one acknowledged
leader. In writing to one group about his concern for a
slave named Onesimus, Paul addressed his letter to three
people in particular as well as to the whole gathering: "To
Philemon our dear friend and co-worker, to Apphia our sis-

ter, to Archippus our fellow soldier, and to the church in your house."[18] Unfortunately, this translation masks the nature of the relationships Paul had with Philemon and Apphia. Here he does not call the woman his *adelphe,* his sister, but rather his *agapetos,* his beloved or dear friend— the same term of affection he used for Philemon. The expression suggests that Paul held women in equal regard, and leadership in an early Christian community could be shared among women and men—among those who considered themselves to be sisters and brothers in a new family. Unfortunately, because of our tendency to want short, easy-to-remember names for things, we have lost sight of the fact that Paul's letter was not addressed just to Philemon. We would have a better understanding of the early church if we always referred to this brief note as the Letter to Philemon, Apphia, and Archippus.

We know nothing more about Chloe, Nympha, and Apphia — but the names of these women in Paul's correspondence give us a picture of life in the communities organized by Paul. In organizing these new communities, he frequently began by recruiting an able woman to be his partner in mission. In describing Paul's collaboration with Lydia, the Acts of the Apostles may be relating more than an isolated event in Paul's missionary activity; perhaps we have an account of Paul's typical method of operation in any new city:

> We set sail from Troas and took a straight course to Samothrace, the following day to Neapolis, and from there to Philippi, which is a leading city of the district of Macedonia and a Roman colony. We remained in this city for some days. On the sabbath day we went outside the gate by the river, where we supposed there was a place of prayer; and we sat down and spoke to the women who had gathered there. A certain woman named Lydia, a worshiper of God, was listening to us; she was from the city of Thyatira and a dealer in purple cloth. The Lord opened her heart to listen eagerly to what was said by Paul. When she and her household

were baptized, she urged us, saying, "If you have judged me to be faithful to the Lord, come and stay at my home." And she prevailed upon us.[19]

In this episode, the people most interested in what Paul had to say were women. At least one of them was "a worshiper of God"—that is, a Gentile who was attracted to Judaism and attended synagogue. Many middle-class people in the first century found the monotheism and personal morality emphasized by the Jews to be more appealing than their traditional religions, but because of the cultural chasm between Jews and Gentiles they had not converted to Judaism. Paul was more successful in recruiting these "God-worshiping" Gentiles than he was in trying to attract Jews to his cause.

The story also emphasizes the wealth Lydia had at her disposal. She was a dealer in the purple cloth that only the very rich could afford, the implication being that, like other dealers in luxury items, she was well off herself. She was also in charge of her own household, a position that suggests she was a widow who had taken over the family business. The other indication that she was a person of consequence is found in her invitation to Paul and his entourage to stay at her house. If she had room for them as well as all those other people whom Paul baptized, the house must have been of good size. With Lydia's house as a base, Paul could gather a community that would continue to meet under Lydia's leadership after he moved on.

Paul acknowledged many such women who were his partners in ministry in the closing lines of his letter to the Christian community in Rome. Unlike the other communities to whom Paul addressed the letters that have survived, the church in Rome owed its founding to someone other than Paul. He had not yet been to Rome so he was introducing himself to the Roman Christians and offering them his credentials. In trying to win the confidence of these people who did not know him, Paul listed nearly two dozen people who could vouch for him. About half of the names on the list belong to women, whom he claims as his benefactors or co-workers in the faith. The most prominent of these, a woman whom he identifies by her nickname "Prisca," we will consider at some length, but the others deserve attention first.

> I commend to you our sister *Phoebe*, a deacon of the church at Cenchreae, so that you may welcome her in the Lord as is fitting for the saints, and help her in whatever she may require from you, for she has been a benefactor of many and of myself as well.[20]

Paul identified Phoebe, the first woman on the list, as a *diakona*, or deacon, and used the masculine form of that term, *diakonos*—sometimes translated as "servant" or "minister" or "co-worker"—in describing the function of men. In other letters Epaphrus and Timothy are called "deacons," and Paul even spoke of himself in the same way.[21] To understand the significance of the term in Paul's vocabulary, we have only to read an earlier portion of his letter to the Romans (15:8) in which he describes Christ as a *diakonos*. Paul believed that Phoebe was one of those who had taken on the work of Christ in the world and who deserved the support of the Romans as she carried on that work.

> Greet *Mary*, who has worked very hard among you. Greet Andronicus and *Junia*, my relatives who were in prison with me; they are prominent among the apostles, and they were in Christ before I was.[22]

Nothing more can be said about the hard-working Mary, but Junia deserves special attention. Some early copies of Paul's letter to the Romans, and until recently most English translations, obscured the importance of Junia by changing her name to Junias and turning her into a man. It seems much more likely that a second- or third-century copyist would substitute a man's name for an apostle with a woman's name than the reverse. It is also obvious why seventeenth-century translators, if they had both options before them, would choose to make the apostle a man rather than a woman. After the death of Paul, the men who attained positions of influence in the church tended to forget that women had ever been acknowledged as their equals.

In Paul's surviving letters, he used the designation "apostle" quite sparingly. In addition to himself, Peter, and James, the brother of Jesus, he names only Andronicus and Junia as apostles. Paul used the word in a technical sense to describe the work of those like himself to whom the risen Lord had appeared and entrusted with a mission, but Luke in writing his gospel and the Acts of the Apostles used the word as an alternate title for the twelve disciples of Jesus.[23] The other three gospels do not employ this anachronistic use of "apostle" for the original company of Jesus's followers, but most of us today are so accustomed to hearing about the "twelve apostles" that we miss the special significance of the term in Paul's writings. Paul was paying Junia the highest tribute available to him when he said that she was "prominent among the apostles."

> Greet those workers in the Lord, *Tryphaena* and *Tryphosa*. Greet the beloved *Persis*, who has worked hard in the Lord. Greet Rufus, chosen in the Lord; and greet *his mother*—a mother to me also. Greet Asyncritus, Phlegon, Hermes, Patrobas, Hermas, and the brothers and sisters who are with them. Greet Philologus, *Julia*, Nereus and *his sister*, and Olympas, and all the saints who are with them.[24]

Paul provided no clues as to why he wanted the recipients of his letter to greet Tryphaena and Tryphosa. Perhaps he feared they would not be taken seriously; their names mean, literally, "dainty and delicate," appellations that do not seem to fit with his description of them as "workers in the Lord." These two, probably sisters, were women operating independently of their families. In fact, if their names suggest what their parents had hoped for them, their mother and father may well have been disappointed that, instead of being decorative objects in the households of respectable husbands, they had become known as "workers in the Lord."

Among those who "worked hard in the Lord" Paul singled out Persis for a mention of special affection. In speaking of her, he used the same term of endearment that he employed when writing to Apphia and Philemon: *agapetos*. To Paul she was not just Persis, but "dear Persis." What people did to win Paul's affection as well as his respect, we cannot say, but his descriptions of them suggest that he was willing to acknowledge distinctions in the relationships he had with a wide variety of people and yet treat them all, women and men, with respect for their abilities and contributions.

The list of greetings in the letter to the Romans illustrates the nature of the church in the time of Paul. Men and women shared responsibility and authority in way that was quite different from the practice of either the Jewish or Roman culture around them. Furthermore, although Paul supported the standard of equality among the sisters and brothers of the new family, he was also sensitive to the unfamiliar problems a Christian community had to face when women were acknowledged leaders. People were used to coping with disagreements among powerful men, but they had less experience in dealing with public quarrels between two powerful women. Such a quarrel between two prominent women in the Christian community at Philippi prompted Paul to write an open letter to the congregation urging the two women to resolve their differences:

> Therefore, my brothers and sisters, whom I love and long for, my joy and crown, stand firm in the Lord in this way, my beloved. I urge Euodia and I urge Syntyche to be of the same mind in the Lord. Yes, and I ask you also, my loyal companion, help these women, for they have struggled beside me in the work of the gospel, together with Clement and the rest of my co-workers, whose names are in the book of life.[25]

Paul's particular admiration for Euodia and Syntyche does not show through the English translation of his words. In English we read that they "struggled beside"

Paul in the work of the gospel. Paul's word was *sunathleo*, based on the same root from which we get our word "athlete," preceded by the word for "with." People in Paul's time most frequently used the word *sunathleo* when they were discussing team wrestling. Paul was saying that these two women were his wrestling teammates. This vivid metaphor pointed both to their strength and to their capacity for cooperation. Paul underscored his assessment of them as his equals when he went on to include them among his "co-workers."

What Euodia and Syntyche were arguing about, Paul did not say. He did not need to explain because their dispute was all too well known among their fellow Christians at Philippi. The argument had so shaken the community that they had written to Paul for advice. The disagreement between the two women had so upset Paul, that in writing he had to work his way slowly to the topic that most concerned him. If you know what is coming at the end, you can read everything in the letter that precedes "Therefore, my brothers and sisters" and see that Paul is carefully laying the groundwork for the unpleasant business that made his letter necessary.

Early in the letter Paul told the Philippians that he wanted to know that they were "standing firm in one spirit, striving side by side with one mind for the faith of the gospel."[26] What was the point of repeating the hope that they were "one" if he did not have information about disunity in the Philippian church? A worry that some people were not working "side by side" must have provoked his comment. A writer would not urge his readers to do what they are already doing without some suggestion that they were to keep up the good work. Paul also suggests that he knows the reason for the discord in the family when he admonishes them: "Do nothing from selfish ambition or conceit, but in humility regard others as better than yourselves. Let each of you look not to your own interests, but to the interests of others."[27] The upset had been caused by at least two people who were bruising egos, and getting bruised in return, during a battle for control of the community's affairs.

Paul was not suggesting that the power struggle had resulted in physical violence, but he still objected to the form in which the fight was taking place. He pleaded with them, "Do all things without murmuring and arguing, so that you may be blameless and innocent, children of God."[28]

Any Christian community could usefully take these admonitions to heart, but Paul must have been thinking about Syntyche and Euodia in particular when he dictated them. Strong women who were not of "one mind," who were not only "murmuring" but also "arguing" about their differences, were upsetting the community. Nothing in their previous experience had prepared any of them, including Paul, for this experience. In Paul's letter, however, we find no hint of retreat from his position that the sisters had as much right to leadership and authority as did the brothers in the new family.

Partners in Ministry

Paul's way of dealing with the problem in Philippi illustrates how well he had absorbed the teaching of Jesus that his followers were to be sisters and brothers, with God alone taking the role of father. Paul rarely speaks in a condescending way about other members of the church. Mostly he calls them sisters and brothers, but he used other terms that also suggest he saw other people as his equal partners in the enterprise. Whether they are men or women, he talks about them as dear friends, co-workers, fellow soldiers, beloved in the Lord, loyal companions, or teammates. Out of exasperation, he may have an occasional lapse, such as when he calls the Galatian Christians "little children," but even then he is urging his readers to grow up and act like adults.

Paul was particularly concerned that the congregations he had founded would continue to recognize women as full partners. When he was defending himself and his companions against charges that they asked too much support from the Christians in Corinth, he wrote:

> Do we not have the right to be accompanied by a believing wife, as do the other apostles and the brothers of the Lord and Cephas?[29]

What Paul meant does not come through as clearly in this translation as in the original Greek. He was claiming that he and his companions had the right to be accompanied on their missionary journeys by an *adelphe gune*. As we have seen, *adelphe* means "sister," and *gune* could mean either "woman" or "wife." So Paul was arguing for the option of having a "sister-woman" or a "sister-wife" as a traveling companion. According to traditions like those embodied in the *Acts of Paul*, a man and a woman leading celibate lives might travel together in the service of the church, as did Paul and Thecla. Or a married couple such as Priscilla and Aquila could tour as a team. Paul called the women companions, whether celibate friends or actual wives, "sisters" because he regarded them as full partners in the enterprise.

Paul insisted that partnership between a man and a woman was common practice in the church. "Sister-wives" or "sister-women" generally accompanied at least three types of men. First, women traveled with the other apostles, people like Paul with a special mission, who had a recognized place in the life of the church. The second group of men who usually had women with them on their journeys were "the brothers of Jesus." Metaphorically speaking, the apostles and Cephas would be included in a group of Jesus's brothers; Paul here must be talking about Jesus's natural brothers, who held an honored place in the church at Jerusalem. And third, even Cephas (also called Peter), who was the most important of the original twelve disciples, traveled about with a woman, presumably his wife, since according to the gospels he had one.[30]

Paul's point was that the status of the women had nothing to do with their being either married or single, but rather with their position as sisters in the new family. As sisters, the women were full partners in the ministry, and as such, deserved the same level of support as the men.

Although many women served the church as partners with men, others collaborated primarily with other women. As we know from Paul's letters and from the Acts of the Apostles, many women in the early Christian communities had no husbands. Some of the widows had broken with their natural families and formed new communities of independent women. For example, Acts tells the story of a "disciple whose name was Tabitha, which in Greek is Dorcas. She was devoted to good works and acts of charity."[31] In describing Peter's visit to her when she fell ill, the story gives us an important glimpse into one aspect of life in the early church. "All the widows stood beside him, weeping and showing tunics and other clothing that Dorcas had made while she was with them." Tabitha's family unit was not a typical household, ruled by a man, but a group of widows who carried out the ministry of Jesus, feeding the hungry and clothing the naked.

Paul respected the independence of both women and men. From his letters we can tell how well he absorbed the teaching of Jesus that he was not to "lord it over" his fellow Christians. He did not create an organization to which he could issue orders and expect them to be obeyed. Instead, he established communities that determined their own direction. He continued to exercise some influence, but he could not dictate policy or doctrine. Just listen to the words he used in the second letter to the Corinthians trying to persuade them that they were on the wrong track:

"We urge you...."
"We want you to know, brothers and sisters...."
"I myself, Paul, appeal to you by the meekness and gentleness of Christ...."
"I wish you would bear with me...."[32]

This is not the language of a dictator or father figure who expects that people will do his bidding, but of someone having an argument with people he respects as his equals.

He will have to convince them of the soundness of his position to get his way. He cannot overwhelm them with personal power. Paul helped make equal partnership between women and men possible because he was willing to treat all of the followers of Jesus as his equals. He dealt with all the members of the church as his brothers and sisters.

Priscilla

From Paul's letters and from the Acts of the Apostles, we can see that the women in the early church held the same positions in the community as did the men. Women were deacons, prophets, apostles, teachers, and leaders of local churches. The only area of church life in which we might wonder about the equality of women with men is in the development of the written record. Until quite recently, everyone took it for granted that all of the written material of the early church was produced by men. Once we see, however, that women were the equals of men in every other respect, the burden of proof that women had not contributed to the writing of the New Testament shifts to those who want to maintain the tradition of male authorship.

Of all Paul's sisters, the best candidate for the authorship of a New Testament work is Priscilla. The Acts of the Apostles describes the first meeting of Priscilla and Paul this way:

> After this Paul left Athens and went to Corinth. There he found a Jew named Aquila, a native of Pontus, who had recently come from Italy with his wife Priscilla, because Claudius had ordered all Jews to leave Rome. Paul went to see them, and because he was of the same trade, he stayed with them, and they worked together—by trade they were tentmakers. Every sabbath he would argue in the synagogue and would try to convince Jews and Greeks.[33]

This was the beginning of a long and rich friendship. The names of the couple appear in the New Testament six times, and four of these times Priscilla's name appears first, a significant indication of her importance in the community.

In the Hebrew Scriptures, books are identified by the name of the leading characters in the books. Except for those who still insist upon ascribing the first five books of the Bible to Moses (a theory that requires Moses to have told the story of his own death), authorship in the Hebrew Scriptures is not a significant issue. Most of the books are collections of oral and written material assembled and worked over by a succession of anonymous editors. As we have seen, at least one of these anonymous editors might well have been a woman, a theologian of the first rank whom biblical scholars know as "J."

With the New Testament, however, there is a shift. All the books of the New Testament are ascribed to particular historical figures except one: the Epistle to the Hebrews. Early editions of the King James Version of the Bible title this book, "The Epistle of Paul to the Hebrews," but that designation has long since been dropped. In the third century, Origen, the great biblical scholar, asked the question, "Who wrote the Epistle to the Hebrews?" and answered, "God alone knows."

Virginia Woolf has alerted us to the possibility that if authorship is anonymous, it may well be that of a woman. Of all the New Testament writings, why does only the Letter to the Hebrews not include the name of the author? All the books of the New Testament canon were to be from the apostolic circle; how did this book of unknown origin get in? At first it did not—the earliest list of the New Testament books did not include it. How did it survive?

The Letter to the Hebrews was probably written toward the end of the first century, in the late 70s or early 80s. Paul had been martyred in the late 60s. A decade had passed, a decade in which the openness of the apostle to women was being challenged by the wave of reaction that crystallized in the pastoral epistles. At this time a woman's name on a letter might have endangered its widespread circulation, but the churches that knew Priscilla would have accepted the letter as an exhortation—a word the letter uses—from her, and they would have kept and cherished it as a word from the apostolic community.

At the turn of the twentieth century, Adolf Harnack, a name well known to New Testament scholarship, propounded the theory that Priscilla wrote the Letter to the Hebrews. Even his great authority, however, was not enough to change very many minds, and those who opposed his theory said that it was not supported by proof.[34] A scholar named Ruth Hoppin, however, was impressed by Harnack's theory and set herself to unearth the proof. Her search took her through ancient Roman records, Scripture, and the catacombs, and she came up with a remarkably convincing thesis, published as *Priscilla: Author of the Epistle to the Hebrews.* "In the nineteen-hundred-year search for a possible author," writes Hoppin, "Barnabas, Apollos, Clement of Rome, and Paul have all been favorite sons. No one thought to look for a favorite daughter, but now the hat of a new candidate is in the ring, and *the hat is a bonnet.*" Point for point, Hoppin shows Priscilla meets every requirement for determining the authorship of the letter, including the necessity for the author to have been well versed in Platonism.

Archaeological finds confirm that Priscilla was a Roman woman born to an aristocratic family. She had converted to Judaism; in the first century Judaism was a missionary faith and attracted many Gentile women because of its proclamation of one God and its high moral standards. And she was married to a Jew. Scholarly and determined, she studied the Hebrew Scriptures, perhaps under the influence of Philo, the Jewish philosopher-theologian who left his native Alexandria and went to Rome in 40 C.E. to defend the Jews accused of failing to honor Caesar. Priscilla, living in Rome, would have had the opportunity to read Philo's works and to talk with him and absorb some of his Platonic philosophy. This possibility alone would account for the Platonic ideas in Hebrews.

Priscilla and her husband Aquila met Paul at a low point in his ministry. He had just had a discouraging encounter with the intellectuals of Athens, in the famous Forum of Areopagus where the philosophers spent their time, says Luke, "in nothing but telling or hearing something new."[35] They found Paul strange and ridiculous. He could make no common ground with them.

It is worth noting that the author of the Epistle to the Hebrews could have made common ground with the Athenian intellectuals by casting the Christian message in Platonic terms. The letter has a two-story view of reality: on the ground floor are shadowy, transient, fugitive events and institutions, while the upper story is the permanent, perfect realm of reality. What human beings need for their salvation is access to the upper story, i.e. to God, "a new and living way. . . through the curtain."[36] These are Pauline ideas, but this is not Pauline language. Did Priscilla hammer out these ideas in long nightly conversations with Paul after the day's work was done? Did she bring her classical education to Paul's passionate training at the feet of the great rabbi Gamaliel? Did she help Paul, scarred by his failure with the Greeks, to become all things to all men?

Priscilla could express her views of the Christian message in her own way, independently of Paul, for Paul did not convert her. According to the story in Acts, Paul found Aquila and Priscilla in Corinth, presumably because he was looking for them. He went to see them because he felt confident that he could stay with them. The only way to account for Paul's confidence in the couple's hospitality is to assume that they were already part of the Christian community. The author of the Letter to the Hebrews claims that the message of salvation "was declared at first through the Lord, and it was attested to us by those who heard him."[37] Because Paul had never heard Jesus, the writer had to have been converted by somebody else. That requirement fits Priscilla, who was already a Christian when she met Paul.

Sharing her house and work with Paul deepened what she already knew. When the time came, she was ready to take on Apollos, a popular preacher, but one who did not have the message of Jesus quite straight. Acts 24:16-18 relates the story:

> Now there came to Ephesus, a Jew named Apollos, a native of Alexandria. He was an eloquent man, well-versed in the scriptures. He had been instructed in the Way of the Lord; and he spoke with burning enthusiasm and taught accurately the things concerning Jesus, though he knew only the baptism of John. He began to speak boldly in the synagogue; but when Priscilla and Aquila heard him, they took him aside and explained the Way of God to him more accurately.

It is hard to see why anyone should assume that Apollos should be preferred as the probable author of the letter, since Priscilla was his teacher. Priscilla had to teach Apollos that the followers of Jesus had more to offer than the baptism of John. The baptism of John was for repentance under the law, but the ministry of Jesus established a new covenant between God and human beings mediated by the High Priesthood of Jesus. The burden of the Epistle to the Hebrews is to make just this point, the point that Apollos had missed and needed to be taught by Priscilla.

Among the greetings with which Paul concluded his letter to the Romans is a greeting to this couple, his dear friends. Once again Priscilla's name is first. This time Paul uses an affectionate diminutive:

> Greet Prisca and Aquila, who work with me in Christ Jesus, and who risked their necks for my life, to whom not only I give thanks, but also all the churches of the Gentiles. Greet also the church in their house.[38]

Priscilla and Aquila were people of means, as attested by the extent of their travels and by the spaciousness of their house. They showed up in Corinth, Ephesus, and Rome. Hoppin believes they came to Rome while Paul was in prison in an effort by Priscilla to use her connections to get Paul freed. Could this be the time they risked their necks? The church in their house is mentioned again in Paul's concluding greeting in the first letter to the Corinthians. That must have been no small house to take in a weary traveler and provide a gathering place for a worshiping community.

The last glimpse we have of Paul and his sister Priscilla is in one of the genuine fragments of Paul in the second letter to Timothy. The apostle is old and sick and in prison. The time of his departure has come, he says, and he sends a final word: "Greet Prisca and Aquila."

Priscilla appears to have been the most influential woman in the early church. As a wealthy person, looking after Paul and the other apostles and opening her house as a place of meeting for a new congregation, she stood in the tradition of those women who supported Jesus of Nazareth out of their own means. She was a recognized philosopher and teacher. She was a partner in ministry with her husband, one of the "sister-wives" for whom Paul expressed such respect in his first letter to the Corinthians. She was also one of the people Paul described as a co-worker, a person he regarded as an equal. Now we can also entertain the possibility that she exercised influence throughout the early church by her letters as well as her visits to congregations. Perhaps more than any other woman in the first-century church, Priscilla set the standard for fulfilling what Jesus had in mind when he declared that his sisters were those who do the will of God.

The Sisters Disappear

By studying the genuine letters of Paul and by reading between the lines of the Acts of the Apostles, we can arrive at a fairly clear picture of the early church. The church under the guidance of Paul in many ways fulfilled the radical vision of a new family proclaimed by Jesus. Its members consistently referred to each other as brothers and sisters in their correspondence and in their stories. Women as well as men led the worship of their communities, offering both prayers and prophecy. Men and women jointly organized and guided some Christian communities, while a woman or a man alone was the key person in others.

Men and women saw themselves as co-workers and partners in ministry. Following the principles established by Jesus, the church had not yet organized itself hierarchically, but women as well as men fulfilled the functions of deacons, teachers, and apostles. Women could live and work independently of men, outside of the normal household arrangement that required a man to be in charge. Finally, we must now add the possibility that a woman as well as a man could write a letter that carried sufficient authority to be circulated among the early Christian congregations

When we come to the letters said to have been written by Paul to Timothy, however, we discover that a radical change has taken place:

> Let a woman learn in silence with full submission. I permit no woman to teach or to have authority over a man; she is to keep silent. For Adam was formed first, then Eve; and Adam was not deceived, but the woman was deceived and became a transgressor. Yet she will be saved through childbearing, provided they continue in faith and love and holiness, with modesty. . . .

> Have nothing to do with profane myths and old wives' tales. . . .

> So I would have younger widows marry, bear children, and manage their households, so as to give the adversary no occasion to revile us. For some have already turned away to follow Satan. If any believing woman has relatives who are really widows, let her assist them; let the church not be burdened, so that it can assist those who are real widows. . . .

> Among [people to avoid] are those who make their way into households and captivate silly women, overwhelmed by their sins and swayed by all kinds of desires, who are always being instructed and can never arrive at a knowledge of the truth.[39]

What happened to the women who were deacons, teachers, and apostles? What happened to the women who worked as partners in ministry with men? What happened to the women who were leaders of congregations? What is this fear of the stories that older women tell? What is this prejudice against widows living independently of men? Where is the respect for women that we saw in Jesus and in Paul?

Dennis Ronald MacDonald has addressed these questions about what happened to the church after the death of Paul in a brilliant little book called *The Legend and the Apostle: The Battle for Paul in Story and Canon.* As the subtitle to his book suggests, MacDonald examined the evidence of recorded legends as well as the New Testament before arriving at his conclusions. He paid particular attention to a second-century document known as the *Acts of Paul*, which includes the story of Thecla, a woman who became a Christian and chose to live outside of a normal household.

Independent women upset the Greek and Roman social system based on the household. Respectable people naturally detested Christians for upsetting the system. By claiming that slaves were the brothers and sisters of their masters, the Christians made themselves suspect; by encouraging independence in women, they forfeited the respect of their neighbors. MacDonald discovered that

> according to the legends, the disruption of the household is not primarily related to the liberation of slaves but the liberation of women. For example, in the story about Thecla, when she becomes a Christian, "those who were in the house wept bitterly, Thamyris for the loss of a wife, Theocleia for that of a daughter, the maidservants for that of a mistress. So there was a great confusion of mourning in the house."[40]

The pressure to conform to accepted social standards proved to be more than the church could stand. Gradually a desire for respectability replaced Jesus's vision of the new family as the guiding principle in the lives of Christians. No longer willing to suffer disrepute in the eyes of their neighbors, Christians began to shape the church in conformity with generally accepted social standards. By the end of the first century, when editors were putting their final touches on the gospels, the blurring of Jesus's vision had already begun. In the middle of the second century, a man seeking immediate respect for his work followed the accepted practice of signing an honored name to his writings. By the time he attached Paul's name to letters supposedly intended for Timothy, the vision of a new family of sisters and brothers had nearly faded from memory.

The vision of the new family had nearly disappeared from memory, but not quite. MacDonald is convinced that even after men had gained control over the church, women were keeping alive the memory of their assertive sisters who once had worked as equal partners with men as they carried out the ministry begun by Jesus. These stories form the core of the *Acts of Paul*, a work that the bishops banned almost as soon as it was written down. Banning the written work was not enough to stop the storytelling, however. The author of the first letter to Timothy was adamant in his denunciation of "old wives' tales," possibly because the stories women told encouraged the notion of their equality with men.

In the twentieth century, Christians who attempt to refocus the vision of the new family do not run the risk of social ostracism that their spiritual forebears did. Gradually, society seems to be moving toward a system that recognizes the equality of women and men. In trying to shape their lives as sisters and brothers, however, Christians may incur the wrath of those within the church who want to perpetuate the attitudes found in the letters to Timothy. For the most part, people who talk about "the Christian family" and about "family values" are ignoring what Jesus said about families. To recover Jesus's vision of brothers and sisters in a new family, Christians will have to refight the battle that was lost in the second century. Perhaps this time Christians who want the church to live up to the standards of Paul will have chance of prevailing.

Endnotes

1. Gal. 3:28.
2. Gal. 4:4.
3. Samples of the New Revised Standard Version translations of *adelphos* and *adelphoi*, where the word stands for a follower or followers of Jesus, are:

> "Why do you see the speck in your *neighbor's* eye, but do not notice the log in your own eye? Or how can you say to your *neighbor*, '*Friend*, let me take out the speck in your eye,' when you yourself do not see the log in your own eye? You hypocrite, first take the log out of your own eye, and then you will see clearly to take the speck out of your *neighbor's* eye" (Luke 6:42).

> "If another *member of the church* sins against you, go and point out the fault when the two of you are alone. If the *member* listens to you, you have regained *that one*" (Matt. 18:15).

> "Be on your guard! If another *disciple* sins, you must rebuke the offender, and if there is repentance, you must forgive" (Luke 17:3).

> "When the *believers* learned of it, they brought him down to Caesarea and sent him off to Tarsus" (Acts 9:30).

> "For those whom he foreknew he also predestined to be conformed to the image of his Son, in order that he might be the firstborn within a large *family*" (Rom. 8:29).

> "Peace be to the whole *community,* and love with faith, from God the Father and the Lord Jesus Christ" (Eph. 6:23).

> "I want you to know, *beloved*, that what has happened to me has actually helped to spread the gospel" (Phil. 1:12).

> "Then I heard a loud voice in heaven, proclaiming, 'Now have come the salvation and the power and the kingdom of our God and the authority of his Messiah, for the accuser of our *comrades* has been thrown down, who accuses them day and night before our God'" (Rev. 12:10).

For a sampling of how the NRSV translates *adelphoi* when the word stands for Jews who are not followers of Jesus, see Acts 1:16; 2:29; 3:22; 7:23, 25; 9:30.
4. Acts 23:16-22.

5. 1 Cor. 14:32a-36. Of course an editor who wanted to bring Paul into conformity with the point of view found in the letters to Timothy may have inserted the words about women that the NRSV translators put in parentheses, but no one has discovered any manuscript evidence to prove this point.

6. 1 Cor. 14:2-3.

7. This was the opinion of Christopher Bryant, author of *Depth Psychology and Religious Belief* (London: Darton Longman & Todd, 1972).

8. 1 Cor. 14:33b-36.

9. 1 Cor. 14:31.

10. 1 Cor. 14:39-40. The NRSV translates "brothers and sisters" as "friends"; the Greek is *adelphoi.*

11. 1 Cor. 11:4-5.

12. 1 Cor. 11:11-12.

13. Jerome Murphy-O'Connor: "1 Corinthians 11:2-16 Once Again," *The Catholic Biblical Quarterly* 50 (1988).

14. Acts 21:8-9.

15. Dennis Ronald McDonald, *The Legend and the Apostle* (Philadelphia: Westminster Press, 1983).

16. 1 Cor. 1:10-11.

17. Col. 4:15.

18. Philem. 1:1-2.

19. Acts 16:11-15.

20. Rom. 16:1-2.

21. Col. 1:7, 23; 1 Corinthians 3:5; 1 Thess. 3:2.

22. Rom. 16:6-7.

23. See Walter Schmithals, *The Office of the Apostle in the Early Church* (Nashville: Abingdon Press, 1969). For Paul's usage, see Gal. 1:11-12.

24. Rom. 16:12-15.

25. Phil. 4: 1-3.

26. Phil. 1:27.

27. Phil. 2:3-4.

28. Phil. 2:14-15.

29. 1 Cor. 9:5.

30. Matt. 8:14-15, Mark 1:30-31, and Luke 4:38-39 refer to Simon's mother-in-law, so at one time he must have had a wife.

31. Acts 9:36-42.

32. 2 Cor. 6:1; 8:1; 10:1; 11:1.

33. Acts 18:1-4.

34. A. M. Hunter, a New Testament scholar at Oxford University, made a scientific guess about the authorship of Hebrews and came up with Apollos, the co-apostle of Paul and friend of Aquila and Priscilla. Apollos was a Jew who had become a Christian; he was an eloquent preacher; he was an Alexandrian; and he was an expert in the Hebrew

Scriptures. In addition he could interpret Christianity in terms of Platonic philosophy. Hunter believes these are the characteristics of the author of the Epistle to the Hebrews. He credits Martin Luther as first seeing this fact. Even Edith Deen, who supports traditional virtues for women, does not accept Harnack's theory that Priscilla is the probable author of Hebrews.

35. Acts 17:21.

36. Heb. 10:20.

37. Heb. 2:3.

38. Rom. 16:3-5.

39. 1 Tim. 2:11-15; 4:7; 5:14-16; 3:6-7.

40. MacDonald, p. 50, quoting from the *Acts of Paul* 3:10.

Chapter 4

Living as Sisters and Brothers in Community

The Bible reveals wisdom to those who follow two disciplines: a study of the Scriptures in their historical context and an examination of their own lives. The life and teaching of Jesus, stories drawn from the lore of the Hebrew-speaking people, and the letters of Paul provide useful guidance at the point where these stories and teachings intersect the immediate concerns of the reader. The Bible passages we have examined suggest many concerns, but we have limited our attention to one point of intersection: our desire to find guidance for women and men trying to relate to each other as equals in church and in society.

Although attitudes toward the role of women seem to be changing, not everyone wants women to have equal access to positions of power or influence. Those who are not interested in equality will not see in the Bible what we have seen, and will not appreciate the importance the early church placed on equality for women. Those who want to bring their lives into conformity with the standard of equality practiced by the first Christians, however, will find valuable guidance in the pages of Scripture if they will examine the practices of their own communities in the light of what they read. Present-day followers of Jesus will be challenged to judge how well they practice equality between women and men whenever they hear about the vision of a new family that Jesus put before his disciples:

"Whoever does the will of my Father in heaven is my brother and sister."

The Trouble with Families

Recovering Jesus's vision of the new family will not be an easy task. The word "family" has negative connotations for many people, especially for those with painful memories of childhood and for those who felt oppressed by a family structure that was outwardly "Christian."

Take Michael, for example. From the time he was a small child, on every occasion that he irritated his alcoholic father, out came the belt. He was so severely beaten for some infractions of his father's rules that he felt the pain for days. No matter how hard he tried, he could not win his father's approval or evoke any sign of affection. Although his sister did not have an easy time of it, either, she was clearly the favorite.

Michael grew up hating his father and resenting his sister. As an adult, he could recall having had positive feelings about his mother, but he also harbored anger toward her for not protecting him from his father's abuse and for denying his father's drinking problem. Michael learned at an early age that much of his life at home had to be kept secret not only from his friends but from his relatives. In spite of his record of being frequently disruptive at school, Michael's grades and SAT scores were high enough to get him into college with a scholarship. His parents gave him a little financial assistance during college, but once he graduated Michael left for the opposite coast so that he could have as little to do with them as possible. People who had such a difficult time growing up often have trouble thinking about family in positive terms.

By talking about their own experience and by studying the Bible with other people, however, even individuals reared in severely disturbed families can find insight and direction through the Bible's stories and images of family. They can recall that as children they could imagine what a kind and loving family would be like, while their hunger for parental love and approval demonstrates their capacity to consider the possible existence of perfect parents. Although they have never seen such parents, they can conceive of another realm in which an ideal parent cares for them and assures them of their worth. According to the Bible, people living in the realm of the everyday world have access to this other dominion, known as the kingdom of God or the kingdom of heaven. Opening their hearts to the ideal parent in the other realm, people can also search in the ordinary world for those who will be their sisters and brothers. Precisely because natural families fail to provide what people need, they may find themselves attracted to the new family represented by the community of the church.

People who long for religion to replace an inadequate or missing father, however, may restrict their own possibilities for developing insight and for coping with the complexities of life. They may have such a romantic view of their heavenly father that for them God becomes exclusively male, and anyone who harbors a vision of such a masculine heavenly kingdom will not be likely to have an urgent desire for equality between the sexes. For example, a bright and well-educated young professional woman attending a conference on inclusive language for worship had always found solace in a vision of God as the perfect male authority. After listening to suggestions for language that would emphasize the feminine aspects of God, she wailed, "You have taken away my father!" In searching for the father she had never known, this woman had limited her view of reality to a male-dominated universe.

Even people who had moderately happy childhood experiences often have trouble with the family image, especially if their parents and the church impressed upon them the importance of the "Christian family." The concept of the Christian family that they learned was in all probability one based on the New Testament letters to Timothy, to the Colossians, and to the Ephesians, in which the father is the head of the household and the mother is subservient and the children owe obedience to both of them. They were brought up on injunctions like "Wives, be subject to your husbands" and "Children, obey your parents."[1] Somewhere along the way, they learned that a woman was the first transgressor and that women could be saved only through bearing children.[2] When the offspring of Christian parents find that the Christian family imagery they learned as children does not work for them as adults, they have a hard time believing that a church might hold another vision of family that is worth considering.

Such families often produce capable daughters who resent the pious Christian maxims that were used to rebuke them for their professional ambitions. Ellen wanted to be a physician, but instead, right after college, she married a member of her church whom her father had chosen to be her husband. On the day of her wedding she had terrible misgivings about marrying a man she did not care for, but going down the aisle her father patted her hand and said, "Don't worry. The Lord will teach you to love him." After two years of trying to be a good wife, Ellen was miserable. The Lord had not taught her how to love her husband; she felt only contempt for the man she had married. So she left her husband and eventually enrolled in medical school, an act that caused a complete rupture in her relationship with her parents. From that time on, Ellen had difficulty thinking of God as a loving father.

Families like Ellen's also send into the world sons who are not prepared to deal with women as professional colleagues. As businessmen or lawyers they could cope with women as secretaries and receptionists; as scientists, they appreciated the help of laboratory assistants; as physicians, they could work with nurses. They could get along in the world as long as the women were assigned supportive roles. Once women entered their lives as fellow business executives, lawyers, scientists, or physicians, they were in trouble. They had received no training in dealing with a woman as an equal. Even men who have rebelled against the repressive attitudes of their parents do not always have an easy time developing a relaxed and open sense of collegiality with women. For them the idea of the

Christian family poses an obstacle in working out new patterns of relationships at work.

People whose early experience has led them to suspect that all talk of the Christian family was designed merely to subjugate women may find themselves pleasantly surprised if they ever make a serious study of the Bible passages about sisters and brothers. They will find that the so-called Christian family represents only one biblical point of view, and one that is at odds with the teaching of Jesus and the practice of the early church. They will discover that Jesus's new family of women and men working in partnership offered an alternative to natural families, which had a tendency to demean women.

Anyone who grew up in a household that was not the white, middle-class, two-parent American ideal might also have trouble with the concept of the Christian family. An African-American whose parents both worked to keep the family just above the subsistence level might feel condemned by anyone who insists that a mother's only worth comes through bearing children, while the offspring of an Irish immigrant mother who worked two jobs to support herself and three children could easily resent the church's exaltation of one way of life over all other possible arrangements. Those who have a negative reaction to the concept of a Christian family, moreover, are not likely to become open to an alternative view unless they happen to encounter a church that attempts to practice what Jesus taught. Many Christians conveniently ignore what Jesus taught about families, particularly family loyalty: "Whoever comes to me and does not hate father and mother, wife and children, brothers and sisters, yes, and even life itself, cannot be my disciple."[3] But once we discover that "the Christian family" does not exist in the teachings of Jesus or in the writings of Paul, they may be free to appropriate Jesus's vision of the new family.

The picture of family life found in the letters to the Colossians, the Ephesians, and Timothy represents a retreat from the radical teachings of Jesus. Those who use these letters as proof-texts to show that wives should be subject to their husbands and that children should obey their parents conveniently forget that closely attached to such admonitions was the commandment, "Slaves, obey your earthly masters in everything."[4] In other words, the authoritarian social structures upheld in these post-Pauline letters contradict everything that the gospels represent as the teaching of Jesus and everything that St. Paul wrote. Perhaps, however, the people who wrote these later epistles were honestly engaged in a struggle to keep the church from falling into anarchy and disrepute; perhaps they thought that the church needed more structure than Jesus had suggested or Paul provided. They may have had the best of intentions, but subsequent generations have tended to use their words to justify their control over women and children and to ignore the balancing injunctions also found in the letters, such as "Husbands, love your wives and never treat them harshly" and "Fathers, do not provoke your children, or they may lose heart."[5] At least the authors of these letters understood that someone needed to place limits on an authoritarian husband or father.

Jesus taught that people must separate themselves from their families of origin in order to become the people they were intended to be. The necessity for that separation may be more obvious for people whose alcoholic parents abused them or whose religious parents oppressed them, but even people whose parents offered them dependable love must break away to become fully developed human beings. The best of human families can stifle and subvert the potential of individuals. People who come from happy families may be in even more danger than people whose families did not function well because good parents can easily become the ultimate—if not the only—source of affirmation in the lives of their children.

Carolyn loved her mother and father with her whole heart. She could always talk to them about anything that was on her mind. She enjoyed pleasing them with good grades in school and with starring roles in her college theater, but she never felt any pressure to produce outstanding results in order to win or justify their love. She moved to New York after college trying to get a break on Broadway, but gave up the venture after three years and moved back home with her parents. She took an administrative position in her father's construction company and reconnected with childhood friends. For a while she dated regularly, but by the time she was thirty-two, she seemed to have lost interest in men. None of them quite measured up to her father. By then Carolyn's father had established her in her own apartment, but she continued to see him every day at work, and she talked to her mother on the telephone each day that she did not stop by the house. Her parents tried to keep secret their disappointment in her failure to marry and have children, but at times she guessed how they felt. As she was approaching forty, Carolyn became a little restless. She said to herself, "This is my life, and it's not so bad." At the same time, she suspected that she had not yet become herself; she was merely an extension of her parents.

On the advice of a friend, Carolyn made an appointment with a psychotherapist, an older woman who seemed to be both kind and wise. After several sessions with the therapist, Carolyn came to the conclusion that her attachment to her parents had caused her to limit her choices and to inscribe a small perimeter for her activities. Once she understood that she needed some emotional distance from her mother and father, the therapist suggested that she needed a community that could help her make the transition. She needed another kind of family, one that would encourage her independence. The therapist knew of a church that counted among its members many people who were trying to create a healthy distance from their families of origin. Although organized religion had never been an important part of Carolyn's experience, she was willing to give church a try. With the help of the therapist, Carolyn learned about her psychologically damaging attachment to her parents; with the help of the church, Carolyn learned that her family of origin had been a false savior. Although she could not quite bring herself to "hate" her mother and father, as Jesus taught, she did manage to untangle her life from theirs. She developed new interests and made new friends. She kept her job at her father's company, but she managed to carve out blocks of time for herself to be outside of the intimacy of the family circle.

People with family histories like those of either Carolyn or Michael often develop an early enthusiasm for the new family they find in a Christian community. They are able to create some emotional distance from their families of origin, and feel energized by a sense of freedom from the past.

With the help of the church, many people begin sorting out their feelings about God from their feelings about their parents. Often separating emotional reactions to God from early childhood experiences of mothers and fathers proves to be a difficult task. Even when people can make a clear intellectual distinction between parents and God, they find themselves reacting to Bible stories and the symbols in worship as if God were very much like the mother who would never let them have a birthday party or the father who watched their every move. With time and effort, however, people can allow the stories in the Bible and the symbols in worship to shape new feelings about a God who is different from ordinary parents, a heavenly mother or father who grants them both approval and independence.

Their new family not only provides them with a sense that they are children of an ideal parent but also gives them an opportunity for developing mutually supportive relationships with their new sisters and brothers. The members look out for one another's best interests, visit each other in times of illness or grief, offer encouragement and advice when any of their number faces unemployment. They challenge one another at signs of overindulgence in alcohol, or piety, or work. They enjoy each other's company.

Rituals and community practices strengthen the sense of family by encouraging new members to acknowledge each day the tragedy and sorrow as well as the triumph and joy of life. Weddings and funerals take on new meaning as church members experience these rites of passage as family events. Sunday by Sunday, as the community prays for the sick—the young mother with breast cancer or the eighty-four year old widow who broke her hip—they find their lives increasingly bound up with the lives of their sisters and brothers.

As time goes on, however, people like Carolyn and Michael often suffer from the disappointing discovery that their new family operates all too much like the old one. Church people behave just like other people. They harbor guilty secrets. They compete for influence and control in ways that make the most intense sibling rivalry look trivial by comparison. They fail to notice when some of their number may need them the most.

The new family proclaimed by Jesus and the church that bears his name are not one and the same. The church frequently picks up the words of Jesus but not the life that gives power and meaning to the words. With the incisive insight so often characteristic of the Negro spirituals, these verses catch the chasm between word and deed:

> I met my sister the other day—
> She shook a loving hand.
> Soon as my back was turned
> She scandalized my name.

> Do you call that religion?
> I believe.
> Do you call that religion?
> I believe
> The Sabbath has no end.

> I met my brother the other day—
> He shook a loving hand.
> Soon as my back was turned
> He scandalized my name.

Stumbling upon the secrets of the new family can be almost as disturbing an experience for new members as the discovery that their new brothers and sisters gossip about them. For example, near the end of their first year with a new congregation, one couple put together the scraps of information from a variety of conversations and came to the conclusion that the previous pastor had not died of a heart attack, as everyone said, but had hanged himself. No one talked openly about the cause of the minister's death, but everybody who had been around at the time seemed to know and to feel guilty about how the congregation had treated him, with their incessant demands on his time and their refusal of his request for an assistant. In addition to their guilt, some of the older members continued to nurture the anger they felt toward him for undermining the faith of "the young people" by his sinful act of self-murder. Such secrets have a way poisoning the atmosphere of a church family in just the same way that secrets function in a natural family, destroying trust among the members and eroding confidence.

Discovering the secrets of a new family can be disturbing, but coming across the viciousness of internal church politics can be even more devastating. One young professional woman, a single mother, thought she had found the ideal religious community for herself and her five-year-old daughter. The church building was bright and cheerful, and the people she met seemed to be warm and friendly. She found most of the sermons to be interesting and provocative. After she had made a financial commitment to the congregation and joined the church, older members approached her at the coffee hour soliciting her vote for their slate of officers in the approaching election. They wanted her help in gaining control of the church so that they could demand the resignation of the pastor. They admitted to her that the pastor was charming, but they insisted that he was an incompetent administrator and had been wasting church funds. When those supporting the incumbent also approached her, accusing the opposition of being a handful of mean-spirited malcontents, she saw a nasty fight shaping up and was no longer so sure this was the place for her and her daughter.

Being ignored can also cause people to wonder if they have made a wise choice in affiliating with a church. One person penned this note in response to a form letter received by people who had not made a financial commitment, warning them that they were about to be dropped from the roles:

> I find it interesting that the only time the church keeps in touch is when you need to raise money. I never get a "Haven't seen you in church, hope things are going well" letter. In case you're interested in knowing, not only have I been weathering the recession but also health problems. I am probably about $7,500 in hock at this time, although I do foresee things picking up for me. So if pledging is the sole criteria by which one remains a member, I am very sorry to let you know I can't.

All the unhealthy dynamics of a natural family can develop in a church community. Sometimes the destructive tendencies in a congregation prove to be even worse than what people experience in their own households. Rabbi Edwin Friedman, a family systems therapist, thinks that churches often behave like the sickest of families because they have become a catch-basin for anxiety. The members of most natural families in today's world live great distances apart from one another, giving them little opportunity to work out their difficulties with each other. They bring these unresolved conflicts to the church, often transferring to the minister their feelings of disappointment in their parents. Even congregations that do not employ family metaphors in describing themselves carry on much like people who are related to each other by birth or marriage. Friedman vividly described such congregational dynamics in his widely-acclaimed book, *Generation to Generation: Family Process in Church and Synagogue.*[6]

When they find out that the church is just like any other human institution, including the families from which they came, many people give up and move out. Others come to the realization that although the church can never be the new family that they have always longed for, a congregation can provide an arena in which they may find encouragement for holding to a vision of the way they know family life ought to be lived. The church can also help people examine their longings for an ideal family, assisting them with the task of separating fantasies born of desperation from expectations grounded in reality.

Equality, Justice, Intimacy

Making a distinction between the family of God and the local congregation often proves to be difficult for people who think that they have at last found a place where they can belong, but they are bound to be disappointed unless they learn the difference between the two. The new family that Jesus announced belongs to the realm of the heavenly father, the realm to which we have access now through myth, poetry, and symbol. While these myths, poems, and symbols describe a realm that is not of this world, they also provide ways of interpreting our history as well as our present experiences. As we learn to use the language of the other realm to name our fleeting experiences of being in God's family while part of the church, we become able to name such experiences wherever we live and work. Although we may get glimpses of God's realm through interaction with people in a congregation, the local church will always be a human institution with human failings. Local congregations that are conscious of their failings, however, know that they have been called to do the will of the Father, so they pray at all times that they may behave like the family of God: "Thy kingdom come, thy will be done, on earth as it is in heaven."

Even while it fails to live up to the vision of the new family that Jesus proclaimed, the church has much to offer. For one thing, it keeps the vision alive by telling and retelling the stories of sisters and their brothers found in the Hebrew and Christian scriptures. The Bible puts forward three valuable principles for relationships between women and men: equality, justice, and intimacy without arousal.

The equality of men and women as leaders must have been in the mind of the prophet Micah when he claimed that Miriam as well as her brothers Moses and Aaron had led the people of Israel. Bloom's theory that a woman wrote many of the stories that appear in Genesis and Exodus makes sense when we see that the wisdom of the women she wrote about equaled or exceeded that of men; Rebekah had as much influence over events as her brother Laban, and proved to be wiser than her husband Isaac about the potential of their sons. The churches influenced by Paul practiced this same kind of equality between men and women. The sisters carried out the same functions as the brothers. Men and woman as individuals or as partners presided over congregations. Both women and men prophesied and led the prayers at gatherings of their communities, where both were known as deacons, ministers, and apostles.

In the Hebrew scriptures we find stories of a sister protecting her brother from an unjust system that demanded his life, as well as brothers taking decisive action to provide justice for their sisters. Miriam watched over her little brother Moses to see that he came to no harm, while Dinah's brothers refused to accept her brutal humiliation and rushed to her rescue, just as Absalom destroyed the man who violated his sister. In the gospel narratives, Jesus had the same protective attitude to those whom he regarded as his brothers and sisters, and he warned that he would demand an accounting from those who failed "the least of these" or brought them to harm. He emphasized his concern for justice in a parable about a widow who kept coming to a judge and saying, "Grant me justice against my opponent."[7] She annoyed the judge, who finally gave in, because they both knew that the structure of their community was based on a contractual arrangement that included the right to justice, even for the least important person in the village.

The rules of conduct as well as the stories in the Hebrew scriptures guided the early church in its understanding of its members as sisters and brothers. The metaphor these churches most consistently used to describe their relationship with one another points to the possibility of intimacy without sexual arousal. In healthy families, brothers and sisters can be emotionally, intellectually, and spiritually close without stirring up sexual desires. When the first Christians called each other sister or brother, they were reminding each other not only of their mutual intimacy, but of their acceptance of its limits.

The biblical image of the new family can change the way people behave and treat each other even though the church fails to bring its practices into perfect conformity with the ideal. The real tragedy occurs when Christian communities fail to acknowledge the vision. Without Jesus's understanding of the new family always before them, congregations will unconsciously and complacently slip into the value system of the culture around them. People who become disappointed in a congregation have grounds for hope, however, if they realize that their disappointment has developed partly because the behavior of the members falls so far short of the ideal. Their capacity to compare practice with the ideal means that the congregation in some fashion still holds a vision of the new family. Even the newest member of a church can help bring that vision into sharper focus and help people put into practice what Jesus had in mind for his followers.

When we use the word "practice" in a religious context, we should be aware of the two very different ways we use this word in other areas of life. When a football player talks about practice, he means what he does in order to prepare himself for the real thing, the game that counts. When a lawyer talks about her practice, she means the real thing, her work that counts. In talking about religion, we have to identify which kind of practice we mean each time we use the word. Practicing our Christianity in church is the athletic kind of practice, preparing for the real thing: getting ready to make our work serve God's purpose. Practicing our Christianity in the world where we live and work is the professional kind of practice, what we do that counts. Practicing our religion in church is important insofar as we are preparing for the rest of life where it must be lived.

To suggest that the practice of religion in church resembles a football scrimmage rather than a real game does not mean, however, that the practice can be taken lightly. The injuries a player sustains on the practice field hurt just as much as injuries received in a championship game at the stadium. The point of the practice, however, is to acquire the wisdom and skill that will carry the team to the championship. If the players do not put forth their best effort in a practice scrimmage, they will never be prepared for the day when the score will go into the record book. In the same way, when Christians practice their religion in church, they can easily hurt each other.

Consider the example of Claudia, who decided to take seriously the Christian standard of truth-telling. Having grown up in a household where no unpleasant truth was ever uttered, she knew how easily a family could disintegrate when no one would speak honestly to anyone else. Her new determination to communicate clearly and directly led her one Sunday morning after the worship service to seek out Ben, whose reading of the Bible had bothered her. She told him that he mumbled, that she was unable to hear half of what he read, but she was shocked when Ben, instead of thanking her for her honest critique, became outraged and accused her of trying to undermine his confidence. This had been his first attempt at trying to overcome a fear of speaking in public.

Both Claudia and Ben had inadvertently hurt each other in practicing new forms of behavior in church, but with a little "coaching" from a mutual friend, the encounter was also an occasion for learning. Claudia saw that in trying to manage the anxiety she always experienced in making a direct complaint, she had appeared to be hostile and uncaring in her approach. Ben realized that although she had hurt his feelings, Claudia had shown real courage; she had made herself open to the possibility of being dismissed and rejected. Pain is the price Christians must pay if they are to acquire the wisdom and skill they need to be effective people in their jobs, in their neighborhoods and cities, and in their own homes.

A church that holds up Jesus's vision of a family made up of brothers and sisters living as equals in community provides a good place to practice the forms of behavior the law now demands in most of the Western world. From the fire station to the board room, women now expect men to treat them as equals, but men who have experienced women primarily as mothers or possible lovers are ill-prepared for the circumstances in which they now find themselves. Their primary coping mechanisms are rebellion or domination, neither of which work very well in dealing with a colleague. Many women are also poorly prepared for today's world of work. If they fear the oppressive power of men, they try to disarm them by assaulting them with a sharp tongue or by charming them with a seductive manner. In church, both men and women can experiment with more appropriate forms of behavior by thinking of themselves as adult sisters and brothers.

Women and Men in Partnership

Churches can provide almost unlimited opportunities for women and men to work as partners, like Priscilla and Paul or Apphia and Philemon. Most parish organizations work well with a woman and a man as co-leaders. One congregation, St. Mark's Church in Washington, DC, bases its entire organization on such partnerships. The newsletter has a pair of editors, one woman and one man, each serving two years with overlapping terms so that every editor will have had two partners during the assignment. A man and a woman jointly chair the worship committee. The leaders of the congregation have paired women and men to chair committees working on community concerns and fund raising. Two women and two men direct the Christian education program.

The rector nominated a man to be his associate several years ago, since the associate for the previous eight years had been a woman and he thought a change would be acceptable. However, an open parish meeting showed him that he had failed to perceive a change in the congregation's attitude toward clergy. Men as well as women stood up to testify how much they had come to value seeing a man and a woman face each other as they celebrated Holy Communion at the central altar. "All of humanity must be represented at the Lord's table when we give thanks for the bread and wine," one man asserted. He admitted that he had been upset on a Sunday when the rector was away and two women celebrated communion, but then the idea occurred to him that worship was just as unbalanced if only men played central roles. People testified that in church they wanted their children to see that their daughters had the same opportunities in life as their sons. In other words, the leadership of ritual provides one way that the church holds up the ideal of brother-sister teamwork.

People who bring their children to church come looking for assistance in nurturing them. What the children see during worship will have an impact, but of equal importance is what they experience in their Sunday school classes. To develop a healthy self-understanding, children need both men and women as their teachers, just as Jacob needed the guidance of both his mother Rebekah and her brother Laban. The Rebekah and Laban story can remind single mothers that their children can become overly attached to them and need a strong male influence to bring out the best in them; single fathers are often looking for women with whom their children can form a healthy connection. Even children who live with both of their natural parents can, like Jacob and Esau, easily become more attached to one than to the other. Children of the Jacob type need a masculine influence that their fathers, for whatever reason, cannot supply, whereas those of the Esau type can profit from knowing a woman who accepts them in ways their mothers cannot.

Whenever possible, the directors of an education program would be wise to pair a woman and a man who are unrelated by either birth or marriage to teach a group of children. Married couples often do not make good teaching teams. They usually encounter difficulty in trying to set aside specific times for reflection and planning. If they are going through an awkward period in their marriage, they may have trouble being honest and direct with each other about what is going on in the classroom. Even if their marriage is working smoothly, many couples slip into playing dominant and subordinate roles in teaching. More often than not, the wife dominates and the husband becomes the passive helper. Such an unbalanced partnership looks all too much like an absentee father and a controlling mother, an arrangement which cannot give the young people a healthy sense of equality among men and women in the church family or in society.

When people come into a Christian community where unrelated men and women work as partners in leadership and teaching, they often express understandable anxiety about the possibility of such arrangements encouraging sexual misconduct. The anxiety became so intense for one congregation that they engaged the services of a psychotherapist to help train the teachers in the Christian education program. Working with the expert in human relations, the teachers learned not only to acknowledge the anxiety but also to appreciate the extra energy that arises when men and women work responsibly with each other. The teachers saw that if they ever acted out unsuitable feelings for one another, they would destroy trust both at home and in the community.

Even people who have committed themselves to responsible behavior between themselves and those of the opposite sex often express the need for guidance in figuring out how to behave appropriately. Churches, government agencies, and corporations have been in a frenzy to produce guidelines to limit the possibility of lawsuits over charges of sexual harassment. Some of these codes of conduct have become so detailed and puritanical that they rival Leviticus in their explicit prohibitions. One government agency, for example, absolutely forbids employees to touch each other, even to offer comfort in a time of bereavement.

If Christians pay attention to the earliest tradition of relationships between men and women, they may be able to offer each other, as well as the rest of society, better guidance than a new form of legalism. When in doubt about what to say to a female colleague or how to treat her, a man can ask himself: What would I do if we were a brother and sister who had been reared in an ideal family? What would I do if we were members of a first-century church trying to put into practice Jesus's teaching of his followers to see each other as sisters and brothers, rather than parents and children or husbands and wives. A woman can use a similar test when wondering if a particular joke would be appropriate or if this would be a time to offer an embrace. Would I tell this joke or hug this man if he were my brother and we had grown up with both respect and affection for each other? The sister-brother image is more likely to change behavior in positive ways than any organizational code of conduct.

Organizing as Sisters and Brothers

In addition to providing a way for women and men to practice working as partners, the church also can be a place for modeling a style of leadership based on cooperation rather than coercion, on dispersed authority rather than hierarchy. Jesus cautioned that everyone in the new family was to be a sister or brother and that no one was to take the role of father. Their only father was to be the heavenly one: "You are not to be called rabbi, for you have one teacher, and you are all *brothers and sisters*. And call no one your father on earth, for you have one Father—the one in heaven."[8] The surviving letters Paul wrote to the churches he founded show that he did not control their affairs. Paul obviously thought he could influence their thinking and behavior, but he left them to make decisions for themselves. For example, he could urge the Galatian

Christians to resist the demands of the emissaries from Jerusalem who wanted all of the men to be circumcised, but he had not established structures that would allow him to forbid the circumcision party access to the congregation.

Unfortunately, many ordained clergy have chosen to ignore the gospels and the letters of Paul in developing their understanding of ministry and of church organization. If they do not demand to be called "father," they choose some equivalent honorific, such as reverend, doctor, or pastor. Women clergy have no better record than men in this regard. Although most of the ordained women in the Episcopal Church object to being called either "father" or "mother," they constantly refer to themselves as priests, which sets them apart and over the rest of the people. By insisting on "priest" as a title, they reserve for themselves the function of priesthood that once belonged to the whole community. Writing to the whole church, the author who called himself Peter said, "You are a chosen race, a royal priesthood, a holy nation, God's own people." God has given to all the people, not just the ordained few, the priestly function of making known the mighty acts of God by the way they live their lives.[9]

Although the term is often misused as a way of asserting authority, the church will probably need to continue employing the word "priest" to designate those people chosen to focus their ministries on the organization. Congregations will need some way of identifying those people whose primary concern is the health of the institution, but they will always have to exercise caution to be sure that such identifications do not become the means of setting some of the brothers and sisters over the rest of God's people.

As Jesus described them, the titles and honorifics themselves do not create an obstacle to the development of community; they are symptoms of a deeper problem. Male and female clergy who emphasize their special status by insisting on deferential treatment often betray a lack of confidence in others as well as in themselves. More to the point, by insisting on a parental role for themselves, they show how little confidence they have in their heavenly father to see them through times of anxiety and despair. They rely on status and control, instead of faith, to make themselves feel substantial. They seem to have forgotten what Jesus taught:

> "The kings of the Gentiles lord it over them; and those in authority over them are called benefactors. But not so with you; rather the greatest among you must become like the youngest, and the leader like one who serves."[10]

Clergy who want to control the life of the congregation, like parents of small children, think that they know best. They seldom ask themselves what will be the long-term effect of using titles that cast the members of the congregation in the role of dependent minors and themselves in the role of demanding parents. Then they complain that no one in the congregation will take responsibility, and they are dismayed when the congregation rebels like a group of angry adolescents.

One clergyman who found himself in conflict with the elected leaders of his congregation quoted canon law at great length to prove his right to control the affairs of the church. After he was forced to resign, he found a congregation that suited him much better. They were respectful and called him "father." One congregation rebelled; the other was passive. Often these seem to be the only two options available for congregations who have the misfortune to be led by clergy who demand a parental role in the life of the parish church.

Congregations with authoritarian clergy do have a third option. Rather than fire their ministers or submit to tyranny, they can treat each one as a sister or brother. They can refuse to act as children in the face of a demanding parent. They can allow the ordained person to proclaim God's love and forgiveness in the name of the community, knowing that accepting each other is a function that belongs to them all. They can tell their minister the truth about objectionable clergy behavior without becoming either apologetic or vindictive because they are dealing with an equal, and not a father or mother.

Of course, the clergy are not always to blame for the parental roles they play. Many congregations force their ordained ministers into an authoritarian position because they want to be told what to think, what to believe, and what to do. They believe that training and ordination have put the clergy closer to God and have given them the power to make lay people all right with God. They are afraid that without the clergy as a buffer, they might have to confront God directly, and they develop a tradition of passivity so that they never have to feel responsible and can always blame the clergy when things go wrong.

One such congregation was not at all happy with their pastor when he tried to outmaneuver all their attempts to be dependent on his leadership. He put the question to them bluntly: "Do you mean to tell me that you want me to make all the important decisions?" As they nodded their agreement, some members of the church muttered, "That's what we pay you for." Pushing the issue a bit farther, the minister asked, "And if I make the decisions, will you do what I tell you?" When they all assured him that they would follow his directions, he said, "Fine. Here is what we are going to do. From now on, we are going to share authority and responsibility." Because everyone knew that he had set and sprung a clever trap, his pronouncement did not settle the matter, but the minister discovered he did have ways of slipping out of the parental position into which the congregation kept trying to put him.

To say that clergy are to be the equals of their brothers and sisters in the congregation is not to deny that ordained people have a particular function in the community. Every organization needs at its center someone whose efforts are focused on the organization. This is a presiding function, not a controlling function. Clergy may preside at meetings precisely so that others may speak and make decisions. Clergy may preside at worship so that others may make the best use of their talents. As the Acts of the Apostles relates the story, Peter was the first to fill this presiding function in a Christian community. Peter took the initiative necessary to get things done, but he did not give orders. When the time came to get organized, he did not appoint someone to fill the empty place on the governing council of twelve people; instead, "Peter stood up among the *brothers and sisters*" and proposed that they hold an election.[11] As the story unfolds, members of the congregation freely challenged both the council of twelve and Peter himself. The Greek-speaking Jews who became followers of Jesus demanded and won recognition from Peter and the other leaders for their special concerns.[12] Later, when "the *sisters and brothers* who were in Judea heard that the Gentiles had also accepted the word of God," they demanded an accounting from Peter.[13] The church remembered that Peter presided over the new community, but did not control its life.

Besides presiding, ordained people make a contribution to the life of the family by the means suggested by the term "clergy," which has the same root as "clerk," a person who keeps track of things. One legitimate function of the clergy who operate at the center of the organization is keeping track of people and activities so that the various parts of the community stay connected with each other. Connecting, like presiding, is not a controlling function.

In our experience, clergy who have given up control have not been left without influence in the congregation. Both in teaching formal classes and in advising leaders and planners, they pass along the lore and theology they have gleaned from their studies. Although volunteers may determine the concerns to be addressed in the sermons, the clergy in these churches preach what they honestly think and believe. Although volunteers edit the monthly newsletter, the clergy have regular columns in which to express their views. Although the committees of the church are autonomous, the clergy can make suggestions. In fact, the influence exercised by the ordained ministers of such churches has probably increased in direct proportion to their diminishing control. When lay leaders know that they bear the ultimate responsibility for an activity or a program, they may feel sufficiently secure in their positions to ask for advice.

At St. Mark's, Capitol Hill, our vestry (the board of directors in an Episcopal Church) also has changed its ways of exercising leadership. Instead of thinking of themselves as being in charge of the congregation, the members of the vestry look for ways of supporting the people who produce the church's activities and programs. Much to the surprise of some vestry members, they find they have more energy and enthusiasm for supporting other people than they ever had for trying to control them.

With this supportive form of oversight, the clergy and members of the vestry have come closer than any of their predecessors in being servants of the people who elected them. No one gets to be *the* father or *the* teacher. We advise and teach each other. When people are advising and teaching, they do not have to show off what they know, but instead help the rest of us discover what we know. We can all work together as sisters and brothers, as equal participants in the life of the parish family. Whether this approach to church management will assure the continued growth of the congregation remains to be seen, but we will measure our success more by the standard of participation set by the first-century church than by membership or attendance figures.

"The Least of These My Sisters and Brothers"

According to Matthew, Jesus did not want his followers to limit their concept of the new family merely to each other. He taught them that they had a responsibility for any person in need. Jesus claimed as his sisters and brothers all those people who are hungry and thirsty, sick and in prison, homeless and without adequate clothing.[14] He referred to them as the "least" of his brothers and sisters, presumably because they were the people with the least power, the least prestige, and the least prosperity.

If Jesus did call the outcasts of society his sisters and brothers, he certainly created a problem for those people who heard him say that for him a sister or brother was one who "does the will of my Father in heaven." After the death of Jesus, his disciples established a community that defined itself by its determination to live according to Jesus's teachings about the will of God. This group of people trying to do God's will was to be the new family Jesus had announced. But what were the disciples to make of these people on the margin of society who had shown no interest in Jesus? Their inability to take care of themselves certainly did not prove that they were doing the will of the heavenly father. How could the disciples possibly have thought that Jesus had in mind the helpless and the despised as candidates for the new family?

The people who wrote and edited the gospels appear to have struggled with the contradictory ways in which the church remembered Jesus to have used the brother-sister metaphor. On the one hand, the sisters and brothers of Jesus seemed to be people who had joined the Christian community; on the other hand, anyone in need was kin to Jesus. The only way to embrace the contradiction is to assume that the church is not the new family of which Jesus spoke, but is merely a symbolic expression of Jesus's family. The family of Jesus includes every human being ever born, even those people who never have suspected that they might be children of God or that they might find satisfaction in trying to do God's will. People who are consciously trying to behave like members of Jesus's family have an obligation to think of the people outside the circle as their sisters and brothers whom tragic circumstances have separated from the rest of the family.

The poor have always been a cause of discomfort for the more privileged. We want to hold them responsible for their condition, so we say that the poor are lazy; they are stupid; they like their way of life; they are paying for sins committed in another life; they are here to provide opportunities for the rest of us to do good deeds. Even Jesus is credited with a heartless response to their condition: "You always have the poor with you."[15] People pay little attention to the fact that this verse has been torn out of context; it is meant to be a rebuke of the privileged, not approval of their indifference. Jesus, however, was never indifferent to human suffering. He chose rather to identify with it, and his very identification with the poor has given the privileged another way out—they have romanticized poverty and identified it with holiness. Jesus participated in none of this unreality, nor did the religious tradition that formed him.

The ancient Hebrews long ago understood that the world sufficed for our need but not our greed, and that the cost of some having more than they needed was that others would not have enough for their needs. Their earliest laws included provisions for those at the bottom—fields were not to be gleaned bare because some was to be left for the poor and the homeless.[16] A worker was not to be made to wait for his pay, nor was a debtor's cloak to be kept overnight as pledge for his obligations.[17] The prophets railed against the children of God who lived in luxury and were not disturbed about the sufferings of their brothers and sisters, and an unknown poet shattered the myth that misfortune was due to wrongdoing on the part of the victim. God's will would be done when each one would sit under his own vine and fig tree and none would make them afraid.[18]

Christians put great stock in the words of Jesus, but what did Jesus say? According to the record, Jesus had much to say against the accumulation of wealth and the systems that encouraged the concentration of wealth in the hands of the few. He shocked even his disciples by declaring that it would be easier for a camel to pass through the eye of a needle than for a rich man to enter heaven.[19] "Then who can be saved?" cried his astounded followers, who had been brought up on the theology that held wealth to be a sign of righteousness. Later exegetes explained away the bite of this remark by saying that Jesus was really talking in this passage about a narrow gate into to the city, a gate that, as one New Testament scholar observed, exists only in the minds of Jerusalem guides pandering to rich tourists. A more realistic and perceptive reader of Luke's gospel challenged the leader of the group, "What did Jesus have against the rich?" The leader replied, "The question might just as well be framed, 'What do the rich have against Jesus?'"

Thinking of people in need as our brothers or sisters can provide a way for church people to act more responsibly. It is important to remain mindful that before God we have all missed our high calling. We have participated in, and profited from, a social and economic system that has contributed to the undoing of some of our sisters and brothers. As we learn to treat "the least" of these with respect, we can consider what sort of responses will help these people find independence and self-respect.

Perhaps a well-spoken and nicely dressed young man has presented himself at the church with a request for fifty dollars. He has found a job but cannot begin work the next day unless he has enough money to pay for his new glasses. What are the options? Assume he is a con-artist and shut the door in his face? Show him that you trust him by giving him the money? Or think of him as you would a brother, down on his luck, whom you have not seen for ages? If you take the third option, you will tell him that you are going to need confirmation of his need for assistance. Then you call the optical dispensary and the new employer before taking any other action. In the case of a legitimate request, you give your brother a check made out to the optical dispensary for his new glasses. If the story does not hold up, you do not trouble your brother with advice, which he will not want to hear, nor do you smile at him triumphantly as you expose the attempted scam and show him the door.

If they can find no way in which to be genuinely helpful, at least by recognizing those in need as their sisters and brothers Christians will not handle their frustration and failure by becoming contemptuous or indifferent. They will keep looking for ways to help. In our community, the churches banded together to engage the services of a social worker who had the time and the skill to separate those with a legitimate need from those who had chosen to make their living by conning religious people into giving them money.

Most church groups who want to help those in society who have the least power, prestige, or prosperity eventually decide that sorting out individual requests may be the least effective way of providing them with the protection and justice they deserve as our sisters and brothers. If our brothers and sisters have no place to live, then we must form alliances with other groups to find ways of increasing the stock of affordable housing. If they are hungry, we must join other concerned people in the neighborhood to provide at least one meal for them every day. If a sister has fled a husband who beat her, we must support the organization that will provide her shelter and clothing and help her make a new beginning.

When Jesus spoke about serving "the least of these my sisters and brothers," he was talking about social outcasts, the people with the least prestige, the least prosperity, and the least power. The people who are the least popular in some communities are those who are sexually attracted to others of their same sex. They may not be the least prosperous, but except in major cities such as San Francisco and Washington, gay men and lesbians are among those with the least political power. Many Christians condemn them in the belief that homosexual relationships are contrary to the will of God, saying that they "hate the sin but love the sinner." To tell homosexual people that they love them but do not give them the same respect as heterosexual people, however, does not constitute a loving act. To denounce homosexuals and to deny them the same rights as heterosexuals sets up a climate in which mindless fear and hatred can flourish. Unprovoked attacks on gay men are an indirect result of the climate of fear and hatred unwittingly created by those people who are trying to promote what they believe is the will of God.

Many of the people who want to deny homosexual partners the legal rights as well as the respect enjoyed by married people do so because of their reading of the Bible. Much of what they find in the Bible, however, is a matter of translation and interpretation. To find the truth which waits for us in ancient scriptures is a task which requires a willingness to use the findings of responsible scholars as well as a faithfulness to the good news delivered by Jesus Christ that we are all his sisters and brothers.

Although the Bible actually has very little to say about homosexuality, a survey of Bible passages that touch on the subject has been complicated in two ways. First, all references to the Sodom and Gomorrah stories in support of the view that the Lord God abhors homosexuality rest on a questionable interpretation of Genesis 18 and 19.[21] Second, several references to "sodomites" in the King James Version of the Old Testament are a result of a mistake in translation.[22] With these misunderstandings set aside, we will discover that only five isolated verses in the entire Bible deal with the subject of homosexuality. A careful examination of those verses will show that they deal with issues of cult prostitution and promiscuity and not with stable homosexual partnerships.[23]

The Christian church has supported marriage and family life for centuries, but many people are unaware of the original reasons for this. The first Book of Common Prayer, which was published in 1549, said that the purpose of marriage was "for a remedy against sin and to avoid fornication." Christians had learned by then that promiscuity had a destabilizing effect on society and, although they may not have understood the reasons, they may have also sensed that promiscuity spread infectious diseases. Similarly, in these chaotic times, all people who consider themselves to be sisters and brothers of Jesus have a special interest in promoting households that are stable and in encouraging committed sexual relationships. Christians can offer support to gay and lesbian couples not only as a way of demonstrating their love for all God's sons and daughters, but also as a way discouraging homosexual promiscuity and prostitution.

Whether the people who need help and protection are outcasts because of their poverty or their sexual orientation, the followers of Jesus know that doing the will of the father means continuing the work that Jesus began with the outcasts of society and acknowledging all people—especially those with the least power, the least prestige, and the least prosperity—as brothers and sisters of Jesus, as children of God.

Joining the New Family

If every human being is a child of God and Jesus's brother or sister, then to speak of joining the family sounds redundant and unnecessary. How can you join a family of which you are already a member? The answer indicated by the gospels seems to be that some choice or decision is required of people who want to recognize their place in the family. The Gospel of John puts it this way:

> To all who received him, who believed in his name, he gave power to become children of God, who were born, not of blood or of the will of the flesh or of the will of man, but of God.[24]

Whoever wrote these words had observed that some people had developed a new confidence in God's love for them through encounters with Jesus of Nazareth. Whether they had met Jesus during his life or had experienced his presence long after his death, these people had acquired the power to claim an identity for themselves as God's children.

The same gospel elaborates on that theme in the story of Nicodemus, to whom Jesus said, "No one can see the kingdom of God without being born from above." A puzzled Nicodemus responded, "How can anyone be born after having grown old? Can one enter a second time into the mother's womb and be born?"

> Jesus answered, "Very truly, I tell you, no one can enter the kingdom of God without being born of water and Spirit. What is born of the flesh is flesh, and what is born of the Spirit is spirit. Do not be astonished that I said to you, 'You must be born from above.' The wind blows where it chooses, and you hear the sound of it,

but you do not know where it comes from, or where it goes. So it is with everyone who is born of the Spirit"[25]

The bewilderment expressed by Nicodemus arose from the double meaning of the words for "born" and "womb." These words have both a primary and a symbolic meaning. As the Greek word *adelphos* indicates, natural brothers and sisters come from the same womb. The new sisters and brothers of Jesus also come from the same womb, but in this case the womb is the "Spirit." In the Nicodemus story the author of the gospel warns the reader not to take the family metaphors in Jesus's teaching literally. To be born into Jesus's new family does not require that we actually retreat into our mothers' wombs and start over, an absurd proposition. What is required to find a place in Jesus's family is another kind of birth, a birth "from above," a birth from another dimension of reality. This other dimension of reality extends beyond the realm of logic and confronts us with a mystery that is as elusive as the wind.

John's mention of water along with the Spirit suggests the sacrament of baptism, the ritual by which the church recognizes an individual as a member of the family. If the gospels understood the intention of Jesus correctly, baptism does not make someone a child of God, but provides the community with a way of celebrating the reality of this person's place in the family proclaimed by Jesus.

John's gospel illuminates the nature of the new family once more with an episode recounted near the end of the Passion narrative. From the cross Jesus committed his mother to the care of a disciple whom he loved, establishing a new family: "Woman, behold your son. . . Behold your mother."[26] The word translated "behold" appears in the text in the imperative mood, a command meaning "Now look" or "Recognize." In telling the story, the author urges the reader to join the beloved disciple in seeing the reality of the new family. The intense life of Jesus with his disciples had given family terms new meaning. Shared meals, physical and spiritual journeys together, and experi-

ences of new birth had given the disciples a deeper understanding of the new thing God was doing through Jesus.

When Jesus's ministry became so radical that his family
feared for him—and doubtless for themselves, too—they
sought to bring him back to the established patterns of
their life. Their attempt provoked his startling response,
"Who is my mother, and who are my brothers and my sisters? Whoever does the will of my Father in heaven is my
brother and sister." A commitment and a way of life gave
meaning to the words, not the other way around. By the
way he lived and treated people, Jesus demonstrated what
he meant by sisters and brothers doing the will of the father in heaven. He provided protection and demanded justice for the least of his brothers and sisters. He offered his
sisters the same love and respect he held out to his brothers. He would not be a father to anyone. He was their
brother and offered to them the possibility of being sisters
and brothers for each other.

People who discover their place in God's family may
want to celebrate that discovery with the ritual of baptism
or with a ritual in which they reaffirm their baptism, but
they may well hesitate. They may balk at the thought of
taking up the work that Jesus began. Or they may be willing to make an attempt at seeing all people as their sisters
and brothers but may not find that the church has any
commitment to the work Jesus began. If they say "yes" to
their place in the family of God by joining a church, however, people may find themselves both humbled and exalted. They will be constantly humbled by seeing how far
short they and the rest of the church fall from the standard
Jesus established, and they will be exalted by glimpses of
the new reality Jesus proclaimed. Even in its failures the
church may call up the vision of all people living in community with loving regard for each other.

In using a family metaphor, Jesus reminded his followers that all people deserved their love and respect and that
not one must be lost. In losing sight of their sisters, the
men who dominated the church for centuries blurred the
vision of the new family that Jesus held up for his disci-

ples. If a sister is lost, the whole family suffers. In finding the lost sister, we all—men and women alike—have a renewed opportunity for finding ourselves as members of God's family.

Endnotes

1. Eph. 5:22; 6:1.
2. 1 Tim. 2:14-15.
3. Luke 14:26.
4. Col. 3:22; see also Eph. 6:5.
5. Col. 3:19, 21; see also Eph. 5:25; 6:4.
6. Edwin H. Friedman, *Generation to Generation* (Harper & Row, 1985).
7. Luke 18:2-5.
8. Matt. 23:8-9. For "brothers and sisters" the Greek is *adelphoi*; the NRSV has "students."
9. 1 Pet. 2:9.
10. Luke 22:25-26.
11. Acts 1:15-26. For "brothers and sisters," the Greek has *adelphoi* and the NRSV, "believers."
12. Acts 6:1-6.
13. Acts 11:1-13. The Greek has *adelphoi*, the NRSV, "believers."
14. Matt. 25:37-40.
15. Mark 14:7; Matt. 26:11.
16. For example, see Lev. 19:9-10 and Deut. 24:19-21.
17. See Lev. 19:13 and Deut. 24:12-14.
18. Mic. 4:4.
19. Matt. 19:23-25; Mark 10:23-27; Luke 18:24-26.
20. Gen. 19:5.
21. "Isaiah seems to have considered it the barbarity of their administration of justice (Isa. 1:10, 3:9); Ezekiel, however, thinks of 'pride, surfeit of food, and prosperous ease' (Ezek. 16:49); and when Jeremiah speaks of adultery, lying, and unwillingness to repent (Jer. 23:14) he does not appear to be thinking directly of unnatural unchastity, which would have been expressed differently." Gerhard von Rad, *Genesis* (Philadelphia: Westminster Press, 1972), p. 218.
22. For example, see Deut. 23:17-18; 1 Kings 14:24; 15:12; 22:46; 2 Kings 23:7. Modern versions have come closer to the original meaning of *quadesh* by translating it "male cult prostitute" rather than "sodomite." The word *qadesh*, which literally means "holy one," appears in both masculine and feminine forms.
23. Lev. 18:22; 20:13; 1 Cor. 6:9-10; 1 Tim. 1:8-10; Rom. 1:26-32.
24. John 1:12-13.

25. John 3:1-7.

26. John 19:26-27 (RSV). The NRSV translates the Greek *idou* with the words "here is," an unfortunate choice that eliminates the basic sense of the word, which has to do with seeing.

ADULT BIBLE STUDY

First Bible Study:
Sisters and Brothers in the Gospels

Matthew 12:46-50
The New Family

Preparation

1. What was Jesus doing when his family arrived?

2. What do you think Jesus's mother and his siblings wanted from him?

3. How did they make their wants known?

4. How did Jesus respond to the one who brought Jesus the message that his family wanted to speak with him?

Group Discussion

1. How do you picture the scene?

2. What does the response Jesus made say about his relationship to his natural family? to his disciples? to the crowds?

3. Try to imagine the reactions of the people in the story—the messenger, Jesus's family, his disciples, the crowds—to the pronouncement Jesus made. What do you suppose they thought and felt?

4. What do you think this saying meant to the followers of Jesus in Matthew's time: "Whoever does the will of my Father in heaven is my brother and sister and mother"?

5. What does this episode suggest to you about your relationship to your natural family? to the church? to God?

Matthew 10:34-39
"Not Peace, But a Sword"

Preparation

1. To whom was Jesus addressing these words?

2. What did Jesus have to say about loving members of your family?

Group Discussion

1. Why might Jesus's listeners have thought he came to bring peace?

2. What do you suppose he meant by "a sword"?

3. What do you think it means to be "set against" a member of your family?

4. Under what conditions might a member of one's own household become one's foes?

5. What kind of behavior do you think Jesus expected when he told his listeners to "take up the cross"?

6. The original Greek word for "life" in this passage is *psuche*, sometimes translated "soul," from which we get our word "psyche." Can you describe people you have known who seem to have lost their lives or their souls?

7. What are some of the ways in which loving your family excessively could cause you to lose your soul or your life?

Matthew 23:1-5
Titles and Terms of Respect

Preparation

1. At the time Matthew's gospel reached its present form, the followers of Jesus were in fierce competition with the Pharisees as both groups tried to win converts among the Gentiles. What does Jesus list as the chief faults of the Pharisees?

2. How are the followers of Jesus supposed to be different from the Pharisees?

3. What did Jesus have against titles or other respectful terms of address?

Group Discussion

1. What terms do people use today that are similar to rabbi, father, and instructor?

2. In what ways does the church as you know it resemble the Pharisees as described here?

3. How well do the church people you know follow Jesus's injunctions to avoid the use of titles and other respectful terms of address? What reasons do they have for ignoring this particular injunction?

Matthew 27:55-56, Mark 15:40-41, Luke 8:1-3
The Sisters of Jesus

Preparation

1. All three gospels mention women who "provided for" Jesus. Where did they meet him? How did they happen to meet him?

2. In the first-century church, what would "providing for Jesus" have meant? (See Matt. 25:31-46.)

3. Besides their role as providers, what other traditions are associated with the women named as providing for Jesus — Mary Magdalene, Mary the mother of two disciples, and Joanna? (See Matt. 28:1-10; Mark 16:1-8; Luke 24:1-12.)

Group Discussion

1. What exactly do you suppose these women did for Jesus?

2. How could they have acquired the "resources" they drew on when they were providing for him?

3. What do you think might have motivated these women to follow Jesus and to look after him?

4. In addition to whatever money they spent, what could have been the less tangible costs to these women for supplying what Jesus needed?

5. What significance do you see for our time in the tradition that the women were first to understand that the tomb could not hold Jesus?

Luke 10:38-42, John 11:1-27
Mary and Martha

Preparation

1. In Luke's story, at whose house in Bethany was Jesus made welcome?

2. What does the story suggest about Martha by identifying the house as hers?

3. What else does the story suggest about Martha's qualities?

4. What insights into Martha's character does John's version provide?

5. How do both stories present Mary's personality and interests?

6. In Luke's story, what is the nature of Martha's complaint to Jesus?

7. How did Jesus respond to Martha?

Group Discussion

1. Do you think that Martha's protest was legitimate?

2. How do you think Mary was affected by her sister's request for Jesus's intervention?

3. What was the "one thing" Martha needed?

4. What do these two stories suggest about Jesus's relationship to women? about the relationship he intended for his male followers to have with his female followers?

Second Bible Study:
Locating the Lost Sister in Hebrew Scripture

Genesis 25:19-34, 27:1-45
Rebekah

Preparation

1. What problems did Rebekah have with childbearing?

2. What tribes did Rebekah's twin sons represent in Hebrew tradition?

3. What rights did Esau trade for a bowl of Jacob's lentil stew?

4. What was the purpose of the blessing Isaac wanted to bestow on his eldest son?

5. What might have caused Rebekah to intervene?

6. How did Esau react when he learned his brother had received the blessing intended for him?

7. What was Rebekah's solution to the problem between her two sons?

Group Discussion

1. Describe the two brothers, Jacob and Esau. What do you see as the strengths and weaknesses of each?

2. What could have been Rebekah's reasons for deceiving her husband instead of speaking to him directly?

3. How do you suppose Jacob felt when his mother disguised him as his brother in order to trick his father?

4. How did Isaac react when Jacob presented himself as Esau?

5. What might Esau have been feeling about his mother and father?

6. What could Rebekah's brother Laban provide for Jacob that he could not get at home?

7. What does this account tell us about the storyteller's understanding of how God operates?

8. How does your understanding of God compare with that of the storyteller?

Exodus 1:8-2:10; 15:20-21; Numbers 12; Micah 6:3-4
Miriam

Preparation

1. Look at the first part of Miriam's story. Why did the mother have to hide her baby boy?

2. What would have made it difficult to continue hiding the baby after he was three months old?

3. What was the mother's plan for saving her son?

4. What responsibility did the mother give to the little boy's older sister?

5. How does the prophet Micah's recollection of Miriam's part in the escape from slavery in Egypt differ from the account found in Numbers 12?

6. In Numbers, what was Miriam's challenge to her brother Moses?

7. According to the story, in what way did Miriam offend the Lord?

8. How did Miriam's offense differ from her brother Aaron's that she alone should be punished?

9. What did Moses do for his sister when she was punished?

Group Discussion

1. What thoughts might have gone through Miriam's mind as she watched to see what would happen to her baby brother?

2. How did the sister react when Pharaoh's daughter discovered the baby? What does her reaction tell us about the sister?

3. Turn to Exodus 15:20-21. What do you think the storyteller meant by calling Miriam a "prophet"?

4. How do you picture Miriam and the other women celebrating the victory?

5. Where were the men at this point in the story? How do you think they felt?

6. Which do you think is the more accurate assessment of Miriam—that of the prophet Micah or the account in Numbers 12?

7. How do you feel about the way Miriam and Aaron were treated for a similar offense?

8. What does the concession Moses made in regard to his sister's punishment suggest about how tradition regarded the relationship between the two of them?

9. In what ways do Miriam, Moses, and Aaron remind you of families you have known?

10. In what ways do you think that the brothers and their sister serve as a prototype of the new family proclaimed by Jesus?

Genesis 12:10-20; 20:1-20; 26:1-11
The Sister Wives

Preparation

1. Compare the three stories. What do they have in common?

2. In Egypt only members of the royal family were allowed to contract marriages between sisters and brothers. How might a knowledge of that custom have influenced the development of these stories?

3. Describe the behavior of the patriarchs in each of the three stories. What does their conduct suggest about their integrity?

4. How do the sister-wives conduct themselves under these circumstances? What are your impressions of them?

5. What else do you recall about Sarah and Rebekah? (In addition to reviewing other parts of Rebekah's story, see Genesis 18:9-15 and 21:8-14 for more about Sarah.)

Group Discussion

1. What do the accounts of the sister-wives suggest about the storytellers' attitudes toward women and men?

2. In what ways might these stories inform our understanding of how women and men can work together as partners?

2 Samuel 12; 13; 14:27
Tamar

Preparation

1. What sort of person was King David?

2. How were Tamar, Absalom, and Amnon related to one another? Where did each live?

4. Why did Amnon think it was impossible "to do anything" to Tamar? (See Lev. 18:6,9,11;20:17.)

5. What was Jonadab's advice to Amnon?

6. How did Tamar respond to her father's request that she look after her half-brother?

7. How did Amnon get Tamar close enough to take hold of her?

8. What arguments did Tamar use in trying to persuade Amnon to let her go?

9. Why did Tamar think that David would have agreed to a marriage between two of his children? (Recall the discussion about the sister-wives.)

10. How did Amnon behave toward Tamar after he had forced himself on her?

11. What was Tamar's evaluation of Amnon's behavior?

12. How did Absalom know something terrible had happened to Tamar? Who else could have learned about the incident?

13. What did Absalom do for his sister Tamar?

Group Discussion

1. What kind of example did King David set for his sons?

2. What circumstances would explain how a man might fall in love with his own sister?

3. What does Jonadab's advice to Amnon tell us about Jonadab? about David? about Amnon? about Tamar?

4. In what ways could a knowledge of David's family have influenced the negative attitude of Jesus and his followers toward natural families?

5. In what ways do you think that David's family could have served as a model for the new family that Jesus envisioned?

Third Bible Study:
The Early Church
1 Corinthians 11:2-16; 14:1-36
Praying and Prophesying

Preparation

1. What problem is Paul addressing in Chapter 11?

2. What does this passage take for granted about the conduct of public worship?

3. What other reference to women prophets can you find in the New Testament? (See Acts 21:8-9.)

4. Look closely at verses 3 and 7-9, and then at 11-12. What does Paul propose as the appropriate relationship between men and women?

5. On what does he base each of his opposing perspectives?

6. What concern is Paul addressing in Chapter 14?

7. Why does Paul prefer prophecy to tongues?

8. Look at verses 33b-36. Some people think these verses were added by someone other than Paul. What do you think?

9. What group of people does the author of those lines want to be silent "in the churches"? Under what conditions were they not to speak?

10. Who would Paul like to see prophesying?

Group Discussion

1. Why do you think the issue mattered enough to Paul for him to construct such an elaborate argument in favor of what he takes to be the proper custom?

2. What difference would having both women and men praying and prophesying make to people who were used to seeing only men in leadership positions?

3. What do you think Paul is emphasizing when he begins the transition from one perspective to another with the words, "Nevertheless, in the Lord"?

4. What do think people were doing when they were "speaking in tongues"?

5. What do you think they were doing when they were prophesying?

6. What do you think about the theory that someone other than Paul inserted the passage that begins with the second half of verse 33 and ends with verse 36?

Romans 16:1-16
Greetings

Preparation

1. How many men does Paul mention in this list? How many women?

2. How does Paul identify Phoebe? Look at a variety of translations and at the footnotes for alternate readings. How do you account for the differences?

3. Who else in Paul's letters are identified in the same way? (Check 1 Cor. 3:5; 1 Thess. 3:2; Rom. 15:8.)

4. How are Andronicus and Junia different from the others on the list? Who else does Paul dignify with that designation? (See Gal. 1:11-12.)

5. What reason did Paul give for saying that Mary, Tryphaena, Tryphosa, and Persis were worthy of mention?

Group Discussion

1. What mention of apostles do you find in the gospels of Matthew, Mark, and John? In Luke's gospel and in the Acts of the Apostles, why do you suppose the original inner circle of disciples are called apostles?

2. Why do you think that some ancient manuscripts have Junia listed as "Junius," a man's name?

3. What do you suppose that Mary, Tryphaena, Tryphosa, and Persis did in the church?

4. Why do you think that Paul identified two women by their relationships to men rather than by their names?

5. What does the list of greetings suggest to you about the church in Paul's day?

1 Corinthians 1:10-17
"Chloe's People"

Preparation

1. What was upsetting Paul?

2. From whom had he received the upsetting news?

3. What other women were leaders of Christian groups in Paul's day? (See Col. 4:15 and Philem. 1-2.)

Group Discussion

1. What do you think Paul is implying about a group of Christians by calling them "Chloe's people"?

2. In what ways do you imagine that Chloe's people differed from those who claimed loyalty to Apollos or Cephas?

Acts 9:36-42; 16:11-15
Independent Women

Preparation

1. Who are the people referred to as "they" in verse 37? In whose house was the "room upstairs"? (Hint: see verse 39.)

2. Who are the "saints and widows"?

3. What clues have we been given about Lydia's degree of affluence?

Group Discussion

1. What does the story about Tabitha reveal about her as a person?

2. What does the story suggest about a particular form of Christian community?

3. What does Lydia's story reveal about her as a person?

4. What do you suppose attracted Lydia to Paul?

5. Among those being baptized, who would have been included under the heading of "her household"?

6. If Paul's collaboration with Lydia was at all typical, what does the story suggest about his mission strategy?

Philippians 2:1-4:7
Women in Conflict

Preparation

1. How does Paul describe Euodia and Syntyche?

2. What clues do you find in the earlier parts of the letter that Paul may have been working up to the particular problem the two women posed for the community?

Group Discussion

1. What would prompt Paul to "urge Euodia and Syntyche to be of the same mind in the Lord"?

2. What does Paul's description of Euodia and Syntyche suggest about his relationship to them? about their position in the Philippian congregation?

3. Why do you suppose Paul waited until near the end of his letter to bring up the subject of Euodia and Syntyche?

4. What does Paul's concern for the problem between Euodia and Syntyche tell you about the organization of the early church?

Acts 18; Romans 16:3-4; 1 Corinthians 16:19;
  2 Timothy 4:19
  Priscilla

Preparation

1. Where had Paul been before he met Aquila and Priscilla in Corinth?

2. How did Paul happen to meet them?

3. Turn back to Acts 18. A follower of Jesus named Apollos appears in verse 24. What information about the man does the story include?

4. What was it about the teaching of Apollos that prompted Priscilla and Aquila to take him aside and explain "the Way of God to him more accurately"?

Group Discussion

1. What does this brief account tell us about Aquila and Priscilla's connection to the church?

2. In the letters, what does Paul's use of the diminutive "Prisca" suggest about his relationship to her?

3. In the letter to the Christians in Rome, Paul asks that greetings be sent to the church in Prisca and Aquila's house. What does this designation suggest about the way Christian communities were organized?

4. What do we learn about Priscilla from her ability to explain "the Way" and from Apollos's apparent acceptance of her authority?

5. Why do you think scholars might be reluctant to entertain the idea that a woman could have written the Letter to the Hebrews, as Harnack suggested? Why do you suppose many people automatically assume that anything of religious importance must have been written by a man?

6. What difference would it make to your understanding of the church if someone could prove that one of the letters in the New Testament was written by a woman? What difference would it make just to admit the possibility?

1 Timothy 2:8-15; 4:7; 5:1-16
The Church in the Second Century

Preparation

1. How is the attitude toward women different in this letter from what you have encountered elsewhere in the New Testament? Be specific; cite the places in Paul's letters that contrast with the attitudes you find here.

2. How did the author of this letter try to reconcile his views about women with what Paul wrote and with what the gospels say about the teachings and attitudes of Jesus?

3. Which views on the place of women in the church have had the most influence—those of Paul or those of the man who wrote the letters to Timothy?

Group Discussion

1. What seems to be the primary concern of the author? What do you think was troubling him?

2. How would you account for the change that has taken place between the time of Paul and the writing of this letter?

3. What do you find in the first letter to Timothy on the subject of women that appeals to you? What do you find that is questionable?

Fourth Bible Study:
The Church Today

Preliminary Reflections

1. How do natural families equip their children for the contingencies of life?

2. In what ways do natural families tend to fail their children?

3. What does the church have to offer that a natural family cannot provide?

4. What signs do you observe that the behavior in your church has been influenced by St. Paul? by the second-century views found in the letters to the Colossians, the Ephesians, and Timothy?

5. In your experience, how do churches duplicate some of the worst tendencies of natural families?

6. If you were determined to treat your colleagues at work as if they were sisters and brothers, how would your behavior differ from the norm? How would your behavior be similar to that of everyone else?

7. In what ways does your church help people practice being sisters and brothers? In what ways does your church discourage such practice?

8. To what extent do the clergy you know function as sisters and brothers in the community?

9. How might your church do a better job of fulfilling Jesus's vision of the new family?

Matthew 25:31-46
"The Least of These My Sisters and Brothers"

Preparation

1. Who are those gathered before the Son of man?

2. On what basis does the king in Jesus's story separate people into two groups?

3. Who are the "least" of the king's brothers and sisters?

Group Discussion

1. What do you think the people on the king's right hand will inherit?

2. In what sense are some of the king's brothers and sisters "the least"?

3. Why do you suppose the story describes the plight of "the least of these" four times when once might have been sufficient?

4. What do you think Matthew and other people in the early church made of the story? How do you think they saw themselves in relationship to people who are most like the least of the king's sisters and brothers?

5. How do the people in your church relate to those around them who are most like the least of the king's sisters and brothers in the story?

Gay Brothers and Lesbian Sisters

Preparation

1. Read the following passages: Gen. 19:1-30; Is. 1:10-17; Ezek. 16:44:52; Jer. 23:9-15; 2 Pet. 2:4-10; Jude 5-7. What do you suppose was the sin of the people of Sodom and Gomorrah?

2. In only two verses in the entire Bible do we find homosexual practices specifically prohibited: Lev. 18:22 and 20:13. Read all of chapters 18 and 20, noticing particularly how each chapter begins. What is the purpose behind all of these regulations?

3. Homosexual practices are mentioned in only three places in the New Testament: 1 Cor. 6:10, 1 Tim. 1:10, and Rom. 1:26-27. Read the chapters in which these verses appear. In each case, what is the primary concern of the author? What other objectionable behaviors do the authors of these letters list?

4. What does the Bible have to say about committed homosexual partnerships?

Group Discussion

1. What did you find that the Bible has to say about homosexuality?

2. In responding to homosexual people, what guidance do you think the church can find in the teachings of Jesus?

John 3:1-10
Joining the New Family

Preparation

1. What does the story say about the man who came to see Jesus?

2. What did Jesus say was necessary for seeing the kingdom? What did Nicodemus imagine that Jesus had told him? What accounts for his confusion?

3. What other words with double meanings does John use in this story?

4. What did John assume was necessary to be born from above? (See also the first chapter of John's gospel.)

5. How did Nicodemus react to Jesus's explanation of being born from above?

Group Discussion

1. What do you suppose that Nicodemus wanted from Jesus? What did Jesus think he really wanted?

2. What do you think was John's understanding of the phrase "see the kingdom of God"?

3. In the mixup over Jesus using a word metaphorically and Nicodemus hearing the word in its primary meaning, what was John telling his readers about religious language?

4. Who is the mother of those "born from above"? What is this mother's "womb"?

5. How, then, do you understand the connections among all those born of this same womb?

6. What do you think would have come to the minds of first-century Christians when they heard this last question posed by Nicodemus? What does the question bring to your mind?

7. How does the church help people recognize the dimension in their lives indicated by the metaphor "born from above"?

8. How do you think the church might be more effective in bringing people to an awareness of this dimension of life, in encouraging them to "see the kingdom of God"?

9. What do you see as the connection between the church and the kingdom of God?

Cowley Publications is a ministry of the Society of St. John the Evangelist, a religious community for men in the Episcopal Church. Emerging from the Society's tradition of prayer, theological reflection, and diversity of mission, the press is centered in the rich heritage of the Anglican Communion.

Cowley Publications seeks to provide books, audio cassettes, and other resources for the ongoing theological exploration and spiritual development of the Episcopal Church and others in the body of Christ. To this end, it is dedicated to developing a new generation of theological writers, encouraging them to produce timely, creative, and stimulating publications of excellence, and making these publications available widely, reaching both clergy and lay persons.